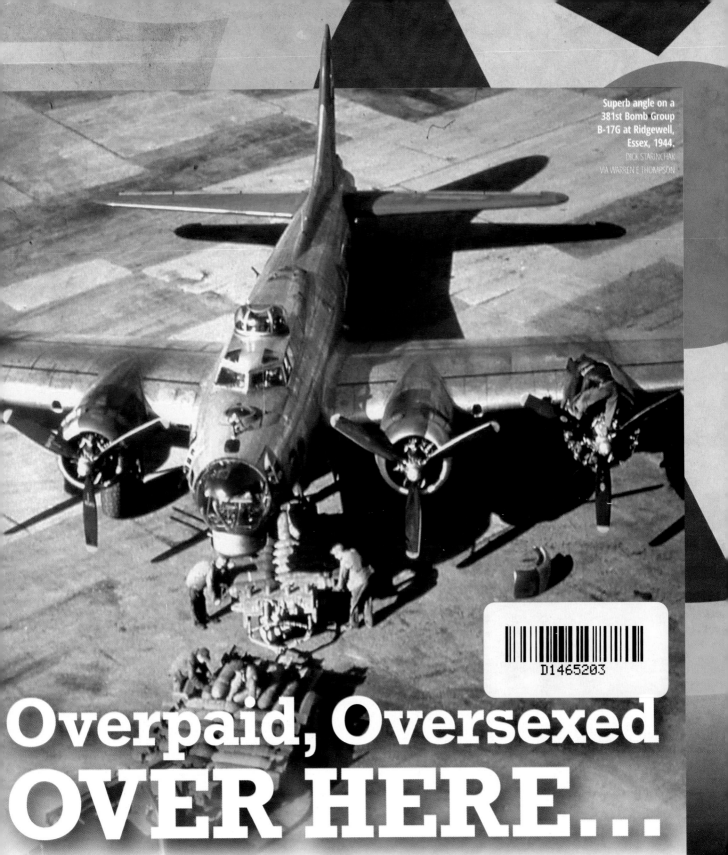

Superb angle on a
381st Bomb Group
B-17G at Ridgewell,
Essex, 1944.
DICK STARINCHAK
VIA WARREN E THOMPSON

D1465203

Overpaid, Oversexed
OVER HERE...

The three 'Overs' is the timeless description of 'Yanks' in the UK. From 1942 GIs, sailors and 'flyboys' began to arrive in Great Britain, they were the first of tens of thousands. The majority of these 'invaders' were also *very* young... or did they just seem that way?

By early 1946 there was hardly a trace of them, and many of the airfields and other establishments that they had inhabited lay silent or had reverted to previous uses. This relatively fleeting stay was to have an effect that has lasted down the generations. They had an impact on the military, political, economic and social thinking, and behaviour of the country.

History has shown that the 'Friendly Invasion' of 1942-1945 was not to be a one-off. As the nature of the 'Cold War' crystallised, the basing of US military personnel in the UK became a reality again in 1948 as

the international situation degraded and the Berlin blockade heralded a tense future. US forces have remained resident, to one degree or another, ever since.

In terms of the USAAF, the 'Yanks' have also left a geographic legacy in the form of the bases from which they flew. The remnants get fewer and fewer with each year, but the attraction of studying and visiting American air bases has not diminished – quite the contrary. The number of museums, visitor centres, trails and memorials continues to increase.

This *FlyPast* special publication aims to show the diversity of USAAF and USAF operations within the UK. As well as the base-by-base, unit-by-unit detail, we aim to convey something of the 'flavour' of the Americans in Britain and pay tribute to the men who found themselves 'Over Here'.

MIGHTYEIGHTH

Compiled, edited and hindered by: Ken Ellis
With thanks to: Steve Beebee, Julie Lawson, Nigel Price, Warren E Thompson and Pete West

Design and layout concept: Dan Jarman
Chief Designer: Steve Donovan
Cover Design: Mike Carr

PRODUCTION
Production Editor: Sue Blunt
Production Manager: Janet Watkins

ADVERTISING AND MARKETING
Advertisement Manager: Alison Sanders
Sales Executive: James Farrell
Advertising Group Manager: Brodie Baxter
Advertising Production Manager:
Debi McGowan
Advertising Production Controller:
Danielle Tempest

Marketing Manager: Martin Steele
Marketing Executive: Shaun Binnington
Marketing Assistant: Deborah Stokoe

Commercial Director: Ann Saundry
Group Editor-in-Chief: Paul Hamblin
Managing Director and Publisher: Adrian Cox
Executive Chairman: Richard Cox

CONTACTS
Key Publishing Ltd
PO Box 100, Stamford, Lincs, PE9 1XQ
Tel: 01780 755131 Fax: 01780 757261
Email: **enquiries@keypublishing.com**
www.keypublishing.com

Distribution: Seymour Distribution Ltd,
2 Poultry Avenue, London EC1A 9PP
020 74294000
Printed by: Warners (Midlands) plc,
Bourne, Lincs

The entire contents of this special edition is copyright © 2013. No part of it may be reproduced in any form or stored on any form of retrieval system without the prior permission of the publisher.

Published by: Key Publishing Ltd
PRINTED IN ENGLAND

KEY

FRONT COVER:
Lt Al Keeler with a 95th Bomb Group B-17G at Horham, 1944.
AL KEELER VIA WARREN E THOMPSON

THIS PAGE:
Evocative image of Europe's only airworthy B-17G, 'Sally B' at a tranquil Duxford. More details of this iconic warbird can be found in the Duxford section.
COL POPE

Contents

Unsinkable Aircraft Carrier

Hard on the heels of Pearl Harbor, US forces flooded into Britain to join the Allied nations, ready to turn the tables in Europe. A staggering number of airfields became USAAF bases. We take you on a journey across the length and breadth of the UK to chart his astounding heritage

About the Airfield Tables

Station:	The vast majority of the USAAF airfields were given administrative numbers. These are often referred to in texts, on memorials, etc.
Location:	Present-day counties and road numbers are given, where applicable.
Previously:	A very *brief* indication of what use the airfield was put to (where applicable) before US forces arrived.
Major Units:	These are confined to units operating aircraft and in general are given only if their period of residence lasted more than three months. Details given include the air force command (Eighth, Ninth and, rarely, Twelfth), group, aircraft types flown, plus constituent squadrons and, where applicable, code letters worn. **Please remember** that most disused airfields have reverted to farmland or other usage. The attitudes of landowners regarding access will vary and readers are urged to seek permission before entering private property. The joy of discovering former airfields is what can be seen, or deduced, from public roads and footpaths!
Afterwards:	Again, very *brief* indication of what use, if any, the airfield was put to after US forces left.

FOR MOST airfields a narrative follows expanding upon the data presented. This also includes details of any museums or other visitor attraction of relevance close by. Occasionally, some venues are dropped in that have no immediate relevance to the USAAF or USAF, but contain subjects of an American 'flavour'. This special edition is based upon a totally revised and expanded version of the series 'Over Here' published in *FlyPast* between 2002 and 2005.

Can't Find An Airfield? Alternative Names

Beck Row	see Mildenhall	**Great Saling**	see Andrews Field	**Rougham**	see Bury St Edmunds
Conington	see Glatton	**Hadstock**	see Little Walden	**Saxmundham**	see Leiston
Flixton	see Bungay	**Holton**	see Halesworth	**Theberton**	see Leiston
Great Chart	see Ashford	**Isle Abbotts**	see Merryfield	**Willingale**	see Chipping Ongar
Great Easton	see Great Dunmow	**Parham**	see Framlingham	**Woodsford**	see Warmwell

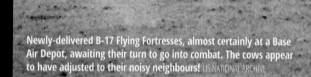

Newly-delivered B-17 Flying Fortresses, almost certainly at a Base Air Depot, awaiting their turn to go into combat. The cows appear to have adjusted to their noisy neighbours! US NATIONAL ARCHIVE

ALCONBURY, Cambridgeshire

Station: 102
Location: North west of Huntingdon, at the junction of the A604 and A1
Previously: RAF from 1938. To USAAF Aug 1942
Major Units: Eighth Air Force, **93rd Bomb Group** – 'Ted's Travelling Circus' – B-24s
Group markings: B in a circle
Codes letters: 328th Bomb Sqn 'GO-', 329th BS 'RE-', 330th BS 'AG-', 409th BS 'YM-'
Eighth Air Force, **482nd Bomb Group** – B-17s and B-24s
Group markings: None
Code letters: 812th Bomb Sqn 'MI-', 813th BS 'PC-', 814th BS 'SI-'
Afterwards: To RAF, 264 Maintenance Unit, Jun 1945, care and maintenance 1948. For USAF use from Jun 1953, see below

THE BASE saw extensive operational use by the RAF until transferring to the USAAF and briefly it was known as Alconbury Hill. Consolidated B-24D Liberators of the 93rd BG were the first to occupy the base, during August to December 1942, followed by the mixed Boeing B-17 Flying Fortress and B-24 equipped 482nd BG – Pathfinder specialists. The 482nd became all B-17 by March 1944. Throughout this time the north-east perimeter of the base – Abbots Ripton – was home to the 35th Air Depot Group, a large maintenance and modification centre.

From June 1953, Alconbury was re-activated as a major USAF base. First aircraft based were the North American B-45 Tornados of the 47th Bomb Wing's 86th Bomb Sqn. The unit later converted to Douglas B-66B Destroyers before moving out in August 1959. The following month, the 10th Tactical Reconnaissance Wing (TRW) arrived with RB-66s. The 10th eventually encompassed three units, the 1st Tactical Reconnaissance Squadron (TRS), the 30th and the 32nd. In 1965 the 1st started conversion to the McDonnell Douglas RF-4C Phantom II. By May 1987, there was only the 1st TRS left when the role changed dramatically. From 1966 to 1972 there was a detachment of the 40th Air (later Aerospace) Rescue and Recovery Wing with Kaman HH-43F Huskie helicopters.

From April 1976 Alconbury became home to the 527th Tactical Fighter Training Aggressor Squadron equipped with Northrop F-5E Tiger IIs for dissimilar air combat training. The unit was 'shortened' to the 527th Aggressor Squadron in 1983 and it left in mid-1988.

The western end of Alconbury, looking south with the A14 in the top right. KEY

In early 1983 the 95th Reconnaissance Squadron, part of the 17th RW, moved in with its Lockheed TR-1 strategic 'spyplanes'. The last of these left in March 1995. From January 1988 the 10th TRW transformed into the 10th Tactical Fighter Wing (TFW) when the 509th and 511th TFSs took delivery of Fairchild A-10A Thunderbolt IIs. From February 1992 the 39th Special Operations Wing arrived with three units, the 6th, 7th and 21st SOSs, equipped with Sikorsky MH-53J Stallions and Lockheed MC-130 Hercules for clandestine operations and long-range rescues. It moved out in September 1994 bound for Mildenhall, Suffolk. The base still has a non-flying USAF enclave, headquartered by Molesworth, but the bulk is used for industrial and storage purposes.

A 1st Gulf War veteran A-10A 'Warthog' outside one of Alconbury's Hardened Aircraft Shelters. KEY-DUNCAN CUBITT

ALDERMASTON, Berkshire

Station:	467
Location:	East of Newbury, south east of the village
Previously:	USAAF from operational, Aug 1942
Major Units:	Twelfth Air Force, **60th Troop Carrier Group** (10th, 11th, 12th, 28th Troop Carrier Sqns) – C-47s
	Ninth Air Force, **315th Troop Carrier Group**, 34th ('NM-') and 43rd ('UA-') TCSs Dec 1942 to Nov 1943
	434th Troop Carrier Group, 71st (CJ-), 72nd (CU-), 73rd (CN-) and 74th (ID-) TCSs, Mar 1944 to Feb 1945
Afterwards:	To civilian use 1946, AWRE from 1949

THE C-47s of the 60th TCG were the first USAAF paratroop aircraft to fly in UK skies, from August 1942. They moved on to North Africa in October 1942. The two Ninth Air Force TCGs that followed were equipped with a mixture of C-47 Skytrains and C-53 Skytroopers, plus CG-4A Hadrian assault gliders. Post-war Aldermaston came to fame as the home of the Atomic Weapons Research Establishment (now the Atomic Weapons Establishment).

ANDOVER, Hampshire

Station:	406
Location:	West of Andover, south of the A303
Previously:	Built for the RFC, opened August 1917
Major Units:	Ninth Air Force, **370th Fighter Group** – P-38s
	Code letters: 401st Fighter Sqn '9D-', 402nd FS 'E6-', 485th FS '7F-'
Afterwards:	Returned to RAF Jul 1944. RAF use to 1976. Army Air Corps from 1977, and still in use as an occasional satellite for Middle Wallop

ANDOVER HAS had a long and almost uninterrupted service connection and has remained all grass throughout. It was the USAAF that gave the station its only spell as an operational airfield with the Lockheed P-38 Lightnings of the 370th Fighter Group, from February 1944. Its pilots worked up for D-Day becoming specialists against radar sites and flak towers. The unit moved with the fighting to Cardonville, France, in July 1944 and the airfield returned to the RAF.

ANDREWS FIELD, Essex

Station	485
Location:	West of Braintree, north of the A120 – also known as Great Saling
Previously:	USAAF from operational, Apr 12, 1943
Major Units:	Ninth Air Force, **322nd Bomb Group** – B-26s
	Code letters: 449th Bomb Sqn 'PN-', 450th BS 'ER-', 451st BS 'SS-', 452nd BS 'DR-'
	1st Pathfinder Squadron
Afterwards:	To RAF Oct 1944, extensive use to Feb 1946

WHILE COMMONPLACE in the Continental USA, Andrews Field was the only US air base to be named after aircrew – in this case Lt Gen Frank M Andrews, Commanding General European Theater of Operations, who had been killed in a B-24 Liberator on 3rd May 1943 during a tour of inspection of US forces in Iceland. Andrews Air Force Base in Maryland was also named after him. As with much of Essex, Andrews Field became a base for intensive B-26 Marauder operations, including a Pathfinder unit. The 322nd left for Beauvais-Tille in September 1944. Andrewsfield (these days one word) remains operational as a delightful general aviation aerodrome.

While the runways have gone at Andrews Field, sections of the perimeter track survive and some are used as minor roads. Looking east, the present grass strip follows the line of the wartime main runway. KEY

ASHFORD, Kent

Station:	417
Location:	South west of Ashford, south of the A28 and north of Shadoxhurst – also known as Great Chart
Previously:	Established as an ALG from Mar 1943 with little use until USAAF arrived
Major Units:	Ninth Air Force, **406th Fighter Group** – P-47s
	Code letters: 512th Fighter Sqn 'L3-', 513th FS '4P-', 515th FS 'O7-'
Afterwards:	Closed by Sep 1944

THE ADVANCED Landing Ground saw some use by the RCAF before the 406th arrived in May 1944, after which it followed the pattern of many such temporary airfields – intense activity then a hasty return to agriculture. The 406th moved out to Tour-en-Bessin, France in July 1944. The post-war car ferry airfield called Ashford has no geographic connection with the ALG.

ATCHAM, Shropshire

Station:	342
Location:	South east of Shrewsbury, north of the village and the B4380
Previously:	RAF. Transferred to USAAF Jun 1942
Major Units:	Eighth Air Force, **31st Fighter Group** – 307th and 308th Fighter Squadrons
	Combat Crew Replacement Center – 6th Fighter Wing
	Eighth Air Force, **495th Fighter Training Group**
Afterwards:	Returned to the RAF Jul 1945. Closed as airfield Apr 1946

ATCHAM MADE its name in the history of the newly-founded US Eighth Air Force in the worst possible way. On June 29, 1942, Lt A W Giacomini became the first of its pilots to perish in the UK when his Supermarine Spitfire crashed on approach. That month, the 31st FG established itself with Spitfire Vs and a variety of support types (with its 309th Fighter Squadron co-located at High Ercall – see below). Major use was by the 6th FW's CCRC and, from October 1943, the 495th FTR – both were tasked with preparing pilots for the demanding conditions of UK's airspace and climate. Main types employed were the Republic P-47 Thunderbolt and Lockheed P-38 Lightnings, which joined the fleet in August 1944. Much of the airfield is now unrecognisable.

As the B4394 wends its way north it cuts through Atcham airfield. The buildings clustered on the left are on the former technical site which is now an industrial park. KEY INSET: **The road from Norton to Walcot was severed to create the airfield. In wartime the A5 trunk road ran to the south, now it hurtles past to the north.** PETE WEST © 2013

ATTLEBRIDGE, Norfolk

Station:	120
Location:	North west of Norwich, south of the A1067, south of Weston Longville
Previously:	Built for the RAF, Jun 1941, extensive use
Major Units:	Eighth Air Force, **466th Bomb Group**, 'The Flying Deck' – B-24s
	Group markings: L in a circle
	Code letters: 784th Bomb Sqn 'T9-', 785th BS '2U-', 786th BS 'U8-', 787th BS '6L-'
Afterwards:	Returned to the RAF, maintenance unit usage then to agriculture. Now a major turkey 'farm'

THE **466th** was known as 'The Flying Deck' – the deck relating to playing cards. The unit operated B-24H, 'J, 'L and 'M Liberators during its tenure at Attlebridge – March 1944 to July 1945. The 466th

Station 120, Attlebridge, looking south. KEY

Bomb Group flew 232 missions and the 785th Bomb Squadron bucked all the trends by flying 55 consecutive missions without loss from going operational in March to July 25, 1944. A substantial memorial is to be found, dedicated in June 1992. At Hethel, Norwich, there is an exhibition devoted to the 446th – see later.

BALDERTON, Nottinghamshire

Station:	482
Location:	South of Newark-on-Trent, south of the village and west of the A1
Previously:	RAF from Jun 1941, heavy bomber training and assault glider storage
Major Units:	Ninth Air Force, **439th Troop Carrier Group** – C-47s, C-53 Skytroopers, Waco CG-4s
	Codes letters: 91st Troop Carrier Sqn 'L4-', 92nd TCS 'J8-', 93rd TCS '3B-', 94th TCS 'D8-'
Afterwards:	Returned to RAF Oct 1944, Bomber Command then storage. Closed 1954. Little remains of the airfield

IN THE 1960s, the A1 moved westwards as part of the massive work to bypass Newark. In so doing it cut the technical site off from the former airfield and much of the hardcore needed for the new road came from the former runways and perimeter tracks. With the Ninth Air Force, Balderton initially acted as a reception point for Troop Carrier Groups. The 439th TCG was based twice, working up here before moving to Upottery, Devon for OVERLORD. Flying Douglas C-47 Skytrains and C-53 Skytroopers and towing Waco CG-4s, the 439th flew in support of MARKET from Balderton in September before moving to Juvincourt, France, later in the month.

C-47 Skytrains of the 61st TCG overfly their home at Barkston Heath. KEC

BARKSTON HEATH, Lincolnshire

Station:	483
Location:	West of the B6403, south of Ancaster, Lincs
Previously:	RAF from Apr 1941, satellite to Cranwell, to the north
Major Units:	Ninth Air Force, **61st Troop Carrier Group** – C-47s, Waco CG-4s, Consolidated C-109s. Code letters: 14th Troop Carrier Sqn '3I-', 15th TCS 'Y9-', 53rd TCS '3A-', 59th TCS 'X5-'
Afterwards:	Returned to the RAF Sep 1945 and operated as a satellite to Cranwell, with occasional gaps, from 1954. Currently the base of the Elementary Flying Training School operating Grob Tutors

OPERATING C-47s and CG-4s from February 1944 and later Consolidated C-109 Liberator tankers, the 61st TCG flew in support of OVERLORD and MARKET GARDEN from Barkston. The 61st moved to Abbeville, France, in Mar 1945 and for two months, Barkston was home to the Curtiss C-46 Commandos of the 349th TCG.

Members of the British 1st Parachute Brigade wait in front of a 14th Troop Carrier Squadron C-47 for the 'off' prior to the Arnhem drop, September 19, **1944.** VIA JELLE MOORTGEN

BASSINGBOURN, Cambridgeshire

Station:	121
Location:	On the A1198, north of Royston
Previously:	RAF from March 1938. To USAAF Oct 1942
Major Units:	Eighth Air Force, **91st Bomb Group**, 'The Ragged Irregulars' – B-17s. Group markings: A in a triangle. Code letters: 322nd Bomb Sqn 'LG-', 323rd BS 'OR-', 324th BS 'DF-', 401st BS 'LL-'
Afterwards:	To RAF July 1945. For USAF use 1950 to 1953, see text. Closed as RAF base (non-flying) Jan 1993

View from the tower at Bassingbourn; a Boeing of a different era – an RAF Chinook – where once the B-17s of the 91st Bomb Group once dominated. KEY-KEN ELLIS

DRIVE DOWN the A1198 – the Roman Ermine Street – and at the main entrance to the former RAF Bassingbourn you will find armoured fighter vehicles as 'gate guardians' as it is currently a major army training camp. Dispersals on the Whaddon (eastern) side of the airfield meant that B-17s could often be seen moving up and down that long, straight road – the most famous of which was B-17F *Memphis Belle*. The B-17Fs of the 91st arrived from Kimbolton in late 1942 and the unit later converted to 'Gs. The 91st had an incredible war, with over 9,500 sorties. From August 1950 another, brief, American era started when Boeing B-29 Superfortresses of the 301st Bomb Group arrived, staying until mid-1951. Also in 1951 RB-50B Superfortresses of the 55th Strategic Reconnaissance Wing took up residence, from January to May. Finally, from mid-1951 into 1952, the B-50Ds of the 97th Bomb Wing made an appearance. Bassingbourn went back to the RAF in April 1953 and became synonymous with the EE Canberra. During the summer of 2012 the Army Training Regiment staged its last parade and it is very likely that the army presence at Bassingbourn will have gone altogether by the end of 2013.

Within the base is the **Tower Museum**, dedicated to all aspects of the airfield's units and including a special exhibition on *Memphis Belle*. Visits to the tower are possible on the second and fourth Sundays of the month, March through to October. Further details on 01763 243500 or take a look at **www.towermuseum bassingbourn.co.uk**

The tower museum at Bassingbourn is exceptional in its content and scope. KEY-KEN ELLIS

Veteran of over 50 missions with the 91st, B-17G 42-97880 'Little Miss Mischief' of the 324th Bomb Squadron, Bassingbourn. PETE WEST © 2013

Eighth Air Force public relations made much of Captain Clark Gable flying missions with the 91st BG out of Bassingbourn in B-17G 'Delta Rebel'. KEC

BEAULIEU, Hampshire

Station:	408
Location:	East of Brockenhurst, between the B3055 and B3054
Previously:	RAF from Aug 1942
Major Units:	Ninth Air Force, **365th Fighter Group** – P-47s Code letters: 38th Fighter Sqn 'D5-', 387th FS 'B4-', 388th FS 'C4-'
Afterwards:	To RAF Sep 1944 and a base for the Airborne Forces Experimental Establishment until 1950. See also below. Returned to heath land 1959

ESTABLISHED ON Hatchet Moor in the New Forest, the P-47Ds of the 365th were followed for a month by the Martin B-26 Marauders of the 323rd BG before the airfield was returned to the RAF. In April 1953 the airfield was reserved for the USAF as a stand-by base, but was never used, returning to the RAF in 1955.

The crew of B-17F 'Memphis Belle' at a formal presentation. KEC

BENTWATERS, Suffolk

Station:	151
Location:	North east of Woodbridge, south of the A1152
Previously:	Built for the USAAF from late 1942. Not taken on, RAF from Dec 1944 until 1950. USAF from Mar 1951
Major Units:	See below for the main unit – the 81st FIG/FBW/TFW. 7554th Target Tow Flight, Douglas TB-26 Invaders Mar to Nov 1952. 87th FIS North American F-86D Sabres Dec 1954 to Sep 1955. 527th TFTW General Dynamics F-16C Fighting Falcons 1988-1990
Afterwards:	Withdrawn as frontline airfield May 1993 but used for exercises. Sold off in 1999 now an industrial estate

INTENDED TO be a USAAF bomber base, Bentwaters had to wait until 1951 to serve the US and from then on became a major base. From September 1951 it was HQ for the 81st Fighter Interceptor Group, with the North American F-86A Sabres of the 91st Fighter Interceptor Squadron resident. In 1952 the nearby airfield of Woodbridge came under the control of Bentwaters and in 1958 the two bases were operated in a unique 'twinned' fashion. In 1953 the 81st converted to F-86Fs and in April 1954 was redesignated as the 81st Fighter Bomber Wing, and converted to nuclear-capable – referred to at the time as 'Special Weapons' – Republic F-84F Thunderstreak in the process. The constituent units were with the 78th, 91st and 92nd Fighter Bomber Squadrons. In September 1958 the unit became the 81st Tactical Fighter Wing and late that year began to receive the superb McDonnell F-101A Voodoo – also a nuclear strike machine. In October 1965 the 81st TFW re-equipped with the McDonnell Douglas F-4C Phantom II, exchanging these for F-4Ds in 1975. Final equipment came in August 1978 with the arrival of the Fairchild A-10 Thunderbolt II (or 'Warthog') tank-buster, and the 81st was expanded to become a six-squadron wing with the addition of the 509th, 510th and 511th Squadrons. A-10s were to be found at Woodbridge as well and at a series of Forward Operating Locations within West Germany. Bentwaters 'Warthogs' took part in the First Iraqi War in 1991-1992 but in May 1993 the last machines left to return to the USA. Apart from some exercises run by USAFE and the RAF, all went quiet.

The **Bentwaters Aviation Society** has developed the **Bentwaters Cold War Museum**. Centred on the Wing Command Post, the incredible displays include the 'Battle Cabin' and the War Operations rooms, which were manned in 1986 during Operation EL DORADO CANYON when UK-based F-111s bombed Libya. Open the first and third Sunday of each month, Easter to October. More details on 07588 877020 or **www.bcwm.org.uk**

The fascinating Bentwaters Cold War Museum is based within the former Wing Command Post. KEY-KEN ELLIS

An F-101C and an F-101A Voodoo of the 91st Tactical Fighter Squadron on approach to Bentwaters. KEC

BIRCH, Essex

Station:	149
Location:	South west of Colchester, south of the B1022
Previously:	USAAF from operational, Apr 1944
Major Units:	Ninth Air Force, storage
Afterwards:	To RAF Jul 1944 – no aviation use. Site now largely gravel pits

THE DISCOVERY of subsidence put paid to Birch's potential career as an operational base. Instead, it was used briefly as a CG-4 glider store with attendant C-47s.

BISTERNE, Hampshire

Station:	415
Location:	South of Ringwood, east of the B3347, east of Kingston, Hampshire
Previously:	Advanced Landing Ground from Sep 1943, but not used
Major Units:	Ninth Air Force, **371st Fighter Group** – P-47s Code letters: 40th Fighter Sqn '9Q-', 40th FS '8N-', 406th FS '4W-'
Afterwards:	Closed Jul 1944

TROUBLES WITH the pierced steel planking-runways at the Advanced Landing Ground meant that Ibsley, Hants, took the P-47s of the 371st for operations April-May 1944, although maintenance was still carried out from the site. The 371st moved on to Beuzeville, France, in June 1944 and the strip was quickly returned to farmland.

BLACKBUSHE, Hampshire

Location:	South west of Yateley, north of the A30, Hampshire
Previously:	RAF from Nov 1942. Civil from 1946. US Navy use 1951 to 1962
Major Units:	See below
Afterwards:	Was civilian/air transport through US Navy use. Remains thriving general aviation airfield

DURING WORLD War Two, the airfield was called Hartfordbridge Flats, but by the time the US Navy used the north-east portion, it was known only as Blackbushe. The US Navy used Blackbushe for communications flying, operating Douglas R4D-8 'Super' Skytrains, but it was also the stopping-off base for a series of exotic recce and intelligence-gathering flights, using Lockheed P2V Neptunes and Martin P4M Mercators. By the late 1960s, the US Navy had moved on, with the comms unit transferring to West Malling, Kent, in 1960.

TOP: **P-47D Thunderbolt of the 352nd Fighter Group's, 487th Fighter Squadron, based at Bodney.**
ABOVE: **'Snoot's Sniper', P-51B Mustang of the 352nd Fighter Group's 328th Fighter Squadron, Bodney, June 1944.** BOTH PETE WEST © 2013

BODNEY, Norfolk

Station	140
Location:	North of the B1108, west of Watton, east of the village of Bodney
Previously:	Built for the RAF as a satellite of Watton – grass runways only from Mar 1940
Major Units:	Eighth Air Force, **352nd Fighter Group** – P-47s, P-51s
Code letters: 328th Fighter Sqn 'PE-', 486th FS 'PZ-', 487th FS 'HO-'

Captain William Whisner was a triple 'ace' in the 352nd Fighter Group's 487th Fighter Squadron. He finished with 15.5 aerial 'kills' during World War Two plus 5.5 MiG-15s over Korea. BILL HESS VIA WARREN E THOMPSON

Afterwards:	Returned to the RAF Nov 1945 and quickly transferred to War Office/Ministry of Defence. Within a major army training area

AN EXAMINATION of a large-scale map will show an almost square-shaped farm track running north from two places off the B1108, with another running parallel to the 'B' road. This marks the extent of the all-grass flying field that was Bodney. In the summer of 1943 the airfield gained pierced steel plank reinforcements in readiness for receiving the 352nd FG. This unit quickly took on the unofficial name of the 'Blue-Nosed Bastards from Bodney'. Initially with P-47D Thunderbolts, P-51B and 'C Mustangs arrived from April 1944, with P-51Ds (and some P-51Ks) from July 1944. Working hard as bomber and tactical strike escorts and very effective target-of-opportunity takers, the blue-nosed Mustangs moved into Belgium to help repulse Germany's Ardennes offensive (the 'Battle of the Bulge') in December 1944, at first settling upon Asch and then Chievres. They were back at Bodney in April, flying their last mission the following month. It was not until November that the last traces of the 352nd disappeared from Bodney.

BOREHAM, Essex

Station:	161
Location:	North east of Chelmsford, north of the A12
Previously:	USAAF from operational, Mar 1944
Major Units:	Ninth Air Force, **394th Bomb Group** – B-26s
Code letters: 584th Bomb Sqn 'K5-', 585th BS '4T-', 586th BS 'H9-', 587th BS '5W-'
Afterwards:	394th to Holmsley South, Hants, Jul 1944. Used by USAAF Air Disarmament Branch to mid-1945. To RAF Apr 1945, closed 1947

TODAY, MUCH of the format of Boreham is visible and used for motor vehicle testing. The tower is still in use and operational with the Essex Police Air Support Unit.

BOTTESFORD, Leicestershire

Station:	481
Location:	North west of Grantham, north of the village of Bottesford
Previously:	RAF Bomber Command from Sep 1941
Major Units:	Ninth AF, **436th Troop Carrier Group** – C-47s
	Code letters: 79th Troop Carrier Sqn 'S6-', 80th TCS 7D-', 81st TCS 'U5-', 82nd TCS '3D-'
Afterwards:	Returned to July 1944, closed to flying late 1945. Storage site until Mar 1960. Much of the airfield and its buildings extant, including the tower

AS A Bomber Command base, Bottesford had an illustrious career being a base for Avro Manchester and then Lancasters. As USAAF Station 481 it was used by C-47s mostly working up for the big airborne 'ops. The 436th arrived in November 1943 and moved to Membury, Berks, and was replaced by the 440th TCG in March 1944 before it moved to Exeter, Devon, the following month.

BOTTISHAM, Cambridgeshire

Station:	374
Location:	On the A14, south east of Bottisham and east of Little Wilbraham
Previously:	RAF from April 1940. To USAAF Dec 1943
Major Units:	Eighth Air Force, **361st Fighter Group** – P-47s and P-51s
	Code letters: 374th Fighter Sqn 'B7-', 375th FS 'E2-', 376th FS 'E9-'
Afterwards:	To RAF late 1944. Closed mid-1946.

THE VERY busy A14 road ploughs right through the middle of Bottisham, which is located south east of the village. The airfield site was sold off by the Ministry of Defence in 1958, but it was not until the new road came about in the 1990s that the site was sliced up and very little survives today. After varied RAF usage, the airfield started

Major Hugh J Nevins in the cockpit of 436th Troop Carrier Group C-47 'War Weary' at Bottesford. Donald Duck is towing a pair of Waco CG-4 assault gliders. KEC

the evolution into Station 374 in late 1943. The 361st FG initially was equipped with P-47D Thunderbolts and then took on P-51 Mustangs, eventually receiving a veritable alphabet of them: 'Bs, 'Cs, 'Ds and even 'Ks. The unit moved out to Little Walden in September 1944, and Bottisham reverted to the RAF, but with little usage.

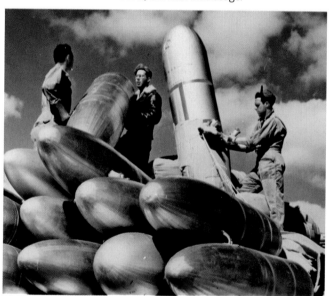

Precious aluminium was diverted to more productive use with the invention of moulded 'paper' drop tanks. Thousands of these were used by the 'Little Friends' of the fighter force as they engaged enemy aircraft, or went low-level to strafe targets of opportunity. US NATIONAL ARCHIVES

High over France, P-51D 'Tika IV' of Bottisham's 361st Fighter Group, 374th Fighter Squadron. RICHARD STARINCHAK VIA WARREN E THOMPSON

P-51D Mustang 44-13410 'Lou IV' as flown by the 361st Fighter Group's commanding officer, Col Tom Christian, from Bottisham, August 1944. © PETE WEST 2013

B-17s returned to Bovingdon in late 1961 for the film of 'The War Lover', starring Steve McQueen. McQueen, playing the obsessive Buzz Rickson flew B-17G 'The Body'. Codes used by the 91st BG at Bassingbourn were chosen for the flying 'stars'. KEC

BOVINGDON, Hertfordshire

Station:	112
Location:	North of the B4505, north west of the town
Previously:	USAAF from operational, Apr 1943
Major Units:	Eighth Air Force, **92nd Bomb Group** – 'Fame's Favoured Few' – B-17s
	Group markings: B in a triangle
	Code letters: 325th Bomb Sqn 'NV-', 326th BS 'JW-', 327th BS 'UX-', 407th BS 'PY-'
	11th Combat Crew Replacement Unit – B-17s
	USAAF Air Transport Command
Afterwards:	To RAF Apr 1946 and also used by BOAC. USAF from Mar 1951 – see below

THE 92nd BG, 'Fame's Favoured Few' operated B-17Fs and some B-17Es from Bovingdon (August 1942 to January 1943) with its first combat mission being staged from the base in September 1943. From March 1951 Bovingdon became a major communications and transport base for the USAF. The base closed in 1976.

Bovingdon, looking towards the south-west. What was the hangar block is now HM Prison The Mount. KEY

BOXTED, Essex

Station:	150
Location:	North of Colchester, west of the A12
Previously:	USAAF from operational, May 1943
Major Units:	Eighth Air Force, **386th Bomb Group** – B-26s with B-26s (May to Sep 1943)
	Ninth Air Force, **354th Fighter Group** – P-51s
	Code letters: 353rd Fighter Sqn 'FT-', 355th FS 'GQ-', 356th FS 'AJ-'
	Eighth Air Force, **56th Fighter Group** 'The Wolfpack' – P-47s
	Codes letters/colours: 61st Fighter Sqn 'HV-', 62nd FS 'LM-', 63rd FS 'UN-'
	65th Fighter Wing air-sea rescue P-47s May 1944 to Jan 1945
Afterwards:	To RAF Sep 1945, extensive use to Nov 1946

INITIALLY AN Eighth Air Force B-26 base, Boxted quickly switched to fighters. The 354th FG was Ninth Air Force administered and flew P-51Bs and then 'Ds and staged the 9th's first-ever P-51B mission on December 5, 1943. The 354th vacated to Lashenden, Kent, in April 1944 with the 8th's flamboyant 56th FG 'The Wolfpack' arriving with Col Hubert A Zemke in command. The unit flew a mix of P-47D Thunderbolts and from early 1945 introduced the P-47M. It moved in September 1945 to Little Walden, before going 'Stateside' the following month.

The **Boxted Airfield Historical Group Museum** is TARDIS-like, punches way above its weight. It tells the story of the 386th Bomb Group and Gabreski's 56th Fighter Group and much more. The group has the rear fuselage of B-26C 41-35253 on loan from the trustees of the Marks Hall Estate at Earls Colne. This is the largest piece of Marauder extant in the UK and is normally viewable on open days. Open on the last Sunday of the month (March to October) and special events. More details on 077747 082085 (museum open hours only) and **www.boxted-airfield.com**

TOP **P-47M Thunderbolt 44-21135 of the 56th's 63rd Fighter Squadron, based at Boxted in the spring of 1945.** PETE WEST © 2013

MIDDLE: **While Boxted earned fame as a home to the 56th Fighter Group, it also hosted Ninth Air Force fighters from the 354th Fighter Group: P-51B of the 355th FS illustrated.** KEY COLLECTION

ABOVE: **The displays within the Boxted Airfield Historical Group Museum pay fine tribute to the airfield's exceptional heritage.** KEN ELLIS

LEFT: **Glenn Miller, playing the trombone, with his orchestra at Boxted.** KEY

Maintenance on B-24H 42-7505 'Old Faithful' of the 446th BG. US NATIONAL ARCHIVES

BRIZE NORTON, Oxfordshire

Location:	South west of Witney, south of the A40
Previously:	RAF from 1937
Major Units:	See below
Afterwards:	To the RAF 1965 and still a major transport and tanker base

IN 1950 Brize Norton was allocated to Strategic Air Command and was given a major transformation to ready it for bombers. The first deployments of Convair B-36 Peacemakers arrived in June 1952. Other types to rotate included B-50 Superfortresses, B-47 Stratojets and B-52 Stratofortresses, plus associated tankers and transports.

BRUNTINGTHORPE, Leicestershire

Location:	North east of Lutterworth, south of the village of Bruntingthorpe
Previously:	RAF from Aug 1942, Bomber Command OTU and other uses until care and maintenance in 1946
Major Units:	USAF Strategic Air Command, 100th Bomb Wing detachments Jan to Jun 1959; USAF Europe 19th Tactical Reconnaissance Sqn Aug 1959 to Aug 1962; also a Base Flight 1959-1962
Afterwards:	Returned to the RAF and used as a reserve airfield. Airfield sold off March 1973 – see below

NOW HOME of the Cold War Jets collection and a variety of other heritage operators, Bruntingthorpe was a busy bomber Operational Training Unit during World War Two. From February 1957 massive engineering work transformed the airfield for use by the USAF's Strategic Air Command. Under the codename REFLEX ACTION, 100th Bomb Wing Boeing B-47 Stratojets were detached to the base. After this the 19th TRS of the 10th TRW (based at Alconbury, Hunts) flew Douglas RB-66 Destroyers from the base for three years.

The **Cold War Jets Collection** is open every Sunday and other collections on the site hold occasional events.
www.bruntingthorpeaviation.com

An RB-66B Destroyer of the 19th Tactical Reconnaissance Squadron taking off from Bruntingthorpe, May 1960. KEC

Modifications to make Bruntingthorpe a base for Strategic Air Command included lengthening the runway and creating extensive aircraft dispersals. KEN ELLIS

Close to the site of the former USAAF Station 125 is the extensive Norfolk and Suffolk Aviation Museum. KEY

Part of the displays at Norfolk and Suffolk Aviation Museum covering Station 125. KEY-KEN ELLIS

A view of the technical area at Bungay in late 1944. KEC

BUNGAY, Suffolk

Station:	125
Location:	On the B1062 west of Bungay – also known as Flixton
Previously:	Built for the USAAF from Sep 1942.
Major Units:	Eighth Air Force, **310th Bomb Group**, 428th BS, B-25Cs Sep-Nov 1942
	Eighth Air Force, **93rd Bomb Group**, 329th BS, B-24Ds Dec 1942-Jun 1943
	Eighth Air Force, **446th Bomb Group**, 'Bungay Buckeroos' – B-24s. Group markings: H in circle. Code letters: 704th Bomb Sqn 'FL-', 705th BS 'HN-', 706th BS 'RT-', 707th BS 'JU-',
Afterwards:	To the Fleet Air Arm and RAF 1945, mostly as storage site until 1950. Disposed of in 1966

BUNGAY WAS home to transitory USAAF units before taking on the 446th BG, which became known as the 'Bungay Buckeroos'. Part of the famed 2nd Air Division, the 446th undertook 273 missions during its stay – a 704th BS machine becoming the first B-24 to achieve 100 missions. The 446th operated B-24Hs, 'Js, 'Ls and 'Ms from November 1943 to June 1945.

A stone's throw to the east of the former airfield is the excellent **Norfolk and Suffolk Aviation Museum** with its aircraft park and extensive display halls, including much on the 446th Bomb Group and the Americans in the area. The oak gates to St Mary's Church were installed in 1986 and presented by 446th veterans, replacing an original set given in 1945. Closed December to February but otherwise open extensively, for more details take a look at **www.aviationmuseum.net**

B-17s, B-24s, P-47s and other types massed at the 1st Base Air Depot, Burtonwood. COURTESY RAF BURTONWOOD HERITAGE CENTRE

BURTONWOOD, Cheshire

Station:	590
Location:	North west of Warrington, astride the M62 motorway
Previously:	RAF – 37 Maintenance Unit. Transferred to USAAF Jul 1942
Major Units:	1st Base Air Depot
Afterwards:	Returned to RAF Jul 1946. See below for USAF and US Army usage

WITH THE M62 motorway thundering across the middle of what was a most impressive airfield, a decreasing amount of Station 590 remains today. With the proximity to the docks of Merseyside and the Atlantic air ferry staging posts, the RAF MU became a specialist in US-built types. When the USAAF was looking for a site for its Base Air Depots, Burtonwood was therefore an obvious choice and the facility was transferred to the USAAF. Station 590, 1st BAD, was the first in operation. Vast numbers of aircraft, engines, systems and spares rotated through the base. By December 1945 it was a shadow of its former self, overseeing the logistical withdrawal of the 'Yanks'.

Burtonwood's Heritage Centre is located on what was Domestic Site 4 of the huge base. KEN ELLIS

The Americans returned in 1948, with Burtonwood and its 'mothballed' facilities proving ideal as a staging post and operational store, and it played a major role in the Berlin Airlift. It became a terminal for Military Air Transport Service (MATS) flights and frequently hosted deployments by Strategic Air Command. Boeing WB-29s, then WB-50D Superfortresses of the 53rd Weather Reconnaissance Squadron were based from 1953 until USAF flying units moved out in April 1959. The MATS terminal transferred to Mildenhall, Suffolk, in 1958.

USAF logistics and other units stayed on until 1965, and in February 1967 the US Army moved in, establishing a massive general depot in support of operations across Europe on the southern portion of the base. The army left in July 1993 and the area has been considerably redeveloped.

The excellent **RAF Burtonwood Heritage Centre** flies the flag for the base's incredible legacy. The centre, to the south of the motorway and on the former domestic Site 4, has amassed an incredible amount of artefacts and images to tell the tale of this great airfield. Open Wednesday to Sunday, follow signs for 'Gulliver's World'. **www.burtonwoodbase.org**

BURY ST EDMUNDS, Suffolk

Station:	468
Location:	East of Bury St Edmunds, close to the A14 – also known as Rougham
Previously:	Built for the USAAF, 1942
Major Units:	Eighth Air Force, **322nd Bomb Group** (450th, 451st, 452nd BSs), Douglas A-20B Havocs and later Martin B-26B Marauders, Jan 1942 to Jun 1943
	Eighth Air Force, **94th Bomb Group** – B-17s
	Group markings: A in a square
	Code letters: 331st BS 'QE-', 332nd BS 'XM-', 333rd BS 'TS-', 410th BS 'GL-'
Afterwards:	To RAF Dec 1945. As well as an industrial estate, elements of the airfield are used by light aviation and the tower is a superb museum.

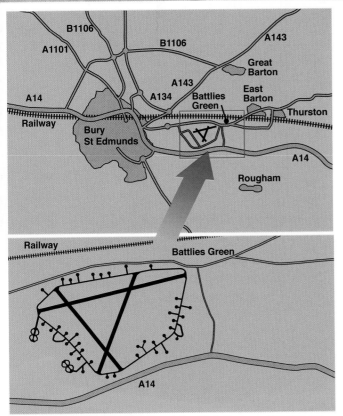

The layout of Bury St Edmunds and its relationship to the town. PETE WEST © 2013

THE MARAUDERS of the 322nd Bomb Group took a pasting during their first missions out of Bury St Edmunds and it was from this that the 8th Air Force decided that the B-26 was of very limited use for its purposes, though of course it was to come into its own with the 9th Air Force. Aircrews of the B-17-equipped 94th BG (June 1943 to December 1945) earned two Distinguished Unit Citations and were to have a long association with the base.

A surprising amount of the former B-17 airfield survives, including the superbly-preserved tower run by the **Rougham Tower Association**: The displays are dedicated to the men as well as the memories of the 322nd and 94th Bomb Groups, and there are poignant memorials and expanding museum facilities – a great place of pilgrimage. Open Sundays, May to October – more details at **www.rougham.org**

BELOW: **B-17G 42-97082 'Mission Mistress' of the 94th Bomb Group's 410th Bomb Squadron. It lost an engine on take-off from Bury St Edmunds on January 6, 1945 and impacted in woods near Moreton Hall, to the west of the airfield. The bomb load exploded, killing five of the crew, four others were injured, as were three locals and damage was caused to housing.** PETE WEST © 2013

CHALGROVE, Oxfordshire

Station:	465
Location:	On the B480 south east of Oxford
Previously:	RAF, non-flying from Nov 1943, USAAF from Jan 1944
Major Units:	Ninth Air Force, 30th Photo Reconnaissance Squadron, Feb 1944; then 10th Photo Group (31st, 33rd and 34th Photo Recce Sqns)
Afterwards:	To RAF mid-1945 and then to Martin-Baker as test airfield

FOR MORE than four decades, Chalgrove has been the spearhead of ejector seat development as Martin-Baker's test airfield, still operating Meteors. The PR units that used Chalgrove operated a variety of types, including photo-configured P-38s and the dedicated Douglas F-3 Havocs, F-5 Lightnings and F-6 Mustangs.

The runways are still used at Chalgrove by Martin-Baker's venerable Gloster Meteor ejector seat test-beds. KEY

CHEDDINGTON, Buckinghamshire

Station:	113
Location:	North west of Ivinghoe, to the south of the village
Previously:	RAF from operational, Mar 1942. USAAF from Jul 1943
Major Units:	2nd Combat Crew Replacement Group, Aug 1943 to Jun 1944
	Eighth Air Force, 858th Bomb Sqn, Jun to Aug 1944
	406th Bomb Sqn, Aug 1944 to Mar 1945
	36th Bomb Sqn, Aug 1944 to Feb 1945
Afterwards:	To RAF (non-flying) July 1945 and closed Feb 1948

APART FROM the B-24 crew proficiency unit, the CCRG, Cheddington's Liberators were all 'spooks', with the units closely associated with the famous 'Carpetbaggers' operating at Harrington in Northamptonshire. The Special Leaflet Squadron B-24s (858th and 406th) were involved with extensive propaganda missions and also in limited support of Special Operations Executive missions. The 36th BS was a Radar Counter Measures Squadron. Post-war the airfield lived a similar 'cloak and dagger' existence for unknown (non-flying) purposes, which explains why so many buildings remain today.

Ragged Irregulars

While its gunners destroyed more Luftwaffe fighters than any Eighth Air Force bomb group, the 91st also suffered the greatest losses. We present a pictorial salute to Bassingbourn's famous B-17s

Douglas-built B-17G 42-107027 'Hikin' for Home' of the 322nd BS ended its time with the 'Ragged Irregulars' ferrying personnel out of North Africa during the summer of 1945. ALL US NATIONAL ARCHIVES UNLESS NOTED

LEAD PIC: **A force of 78 B-17s embarked on a raid to Tours in France on January 5, 1944 – this was the 91st Bomb Group's 100th sortie and it was the first 'Mighty Eighth' group to achieve this. B-17F 42-29837 'Lady Luck' of the 324th Bomb Squadron, with an impressive line of mission tallies on its nose, en route to the target;** ABOVE LEFT: **On its 65th mission, Lockheed Vega-built B-17G 42-97061 'General Ike' of the 401st BS had its starboard inner shattered by flak, ripping away the propeller. This could have been disastrous, but it was repaired and returned across the Atlantic in June 1945;** ABOVE RIGHT: **Gunners of the 91st BG accounted for a record number of Luftwaffe fighters – 420. Personnel of the 91st inspect the damage inflicted on the very vulnerable the ball turret of a Bassingbourn Fortress.**

LEFT: **Assigned to the 91st in June 1944 B-17G 43-37540 became 'Ramblin' Rebel' of the 323rd BS.** USAF VIA WARREN E THOMPSON

BELOW: **A maintenance crew pauses for a moment for an official photo that shows how much 'surgery' was performed on bombers to keep them operational. B-17F 42-29591 'Shamrock Special' suffered damage on return from a raid. Replacing the entire rear fuselage was deemed the best solution for this 401st BS veteran, first delivered to Bassingbourn in June 1943.**

CHELVESTON, Northamptonshire

Station:	105
Location:	East of Rushden, south east of the village of Chelveston
Previously:	RAF from Aug 1941, use included assault glider trials
Major Units:	Eighth Air Force, **301st Bomb Group** – B-17s
	Eighth Air Force, **305th Bomb Group** – B-17s
	Group markings: None
	Code letters: 364th Bomb Sqn 'WF-', 365th BS 'XK-', 366th BS 'KY-', 422nd BS 'JJ-'
Afterwards:	Returned to the RAF, storage site and care and maintenance. See below for USAF use

The crew of B-17F 42-30791 'Pistol Packin' Mama' of the 305th Bomb Group, 422nd Bomb Squadron, Chelveston, February 1944. US NATIONAL ARCHIVES

C-47s of the 60th TCG were the first major US unit, spending a brief period at Chelveston from June 1942. The Boeing B-17F Flying Fortress-equipped 301st BG was a 12th Air Force unit in the care of the 8th, transiting to North Africa. From December 1942 the 305th, with B-17Fs and then 'Gs, established an incredible war record. During OVERLORD it hit V-sites and major installations. It returned to the States in July 1945. In a similar manner to Bruntingthorpe, Chelveston was re-engineered in the mid-1950s ready for Strategic Air Command deployments. From January to June 1959 the base reverberated to the sound B-47s on REFLEX ALERT deployments. Beyond this came RB-66s of the 10th TRW's 42nd TRS, August 1959 to August 1962. Few traces of the base remain, although there is still a US communications enclave within the site.

Bound for Villacoublay in France, B-17Gs of Chelveston's 305th Bomb Group, 366th Bomb Squadron, high above the cloud cover, August 1943. US NATIONAL ARCHIVES

Mustang in a tower

Lt Hans J Grasshoff poses with 'Little Zippie' at Wattisham. KEC

⭐ At Point Clear, Clacton-on-Sea, Essex, inside an historic Martello tower is the East Essex Aviation Museum and Museum of the 1940s. 'Star' exhibit is the salvaged forward fuselage of Wattisham-based 479th Fighter Group P-51D Mustang 44-14574 'Little Zippie'. This machine crashed off the Clacton shore on January 13, 1945 and provides a poignant 'Little Friends' exhibit. Open on Sundays, April to October, with addition times in the summer season.
More details at www.eastessexaviationsociety.org

CHILBOLTON, Hampshire

Station:	404
Location:	South of Chilbolton, east of the A3057
Previously:	RAF from Sep 1940. USAAF from Dec 1943
Major Units:	Ninth Air Force, **368th Fighter Group** – P-47s
	Code letters: 395th Fighter Sqn 'A7-', 396th FS 'C2-', 397th FS 'D3-'
Afterwards:	Returned to the RAF Mar 1945, Vickers-Supermarine test flight centre from early 1947 and likewise Folland from 1953. Closed 1961. Major radio observatory from 1967. Light aviation to date

AFTER THE ground-attack P-47s of the 368th moved out to Cardonville in June 1944 – the first Ninth Air Force P-47s to move to France – a major detachment of the 442nd TCG with its Douglas C-47 Skytrains moved in for casualty evacuation and also for Operation MARKET. Chilbolton remained a USAAF 'casevac' station until the RAF returned.

CHIPPING ONGAR, Essex

Station	162
Location:	West of Chelmsford, north of the A414 at High Ongar – also known as Willingale
Previously:	USAAF from operational, Jun 1943
Major Units:	Ninth Air Force, **387th Bomb Group** – B-26s Code letters: 556th Bomb Sqn 'FW-', 557th BS 'KS-', 558th BS 'KX-', 559th BS 'TQ-'
Afterwards:	To RAF Apr 1945, no operational use. Little of the airfield remains

BUILT BY the Americans, Chipping Ongar was operational from June 1943. The Marauders of the 387th Bomb Group earned a reputation as bridge busters. The 387th moved on to Stoney Cross, Hampshire, in July 1944. Beyond this the airfield became a storage park for Waco CG-4 assault gliders.

CHRISTCHURCH, Dorset

Station:	416
Location:	North east of Christchurch Harbour, north of Mudeford
Previously:	Civil from 1935. RAF from 1940, becoming a shadow factory run by Airspeed
Major Units:	Ninth Air Force, **405th Fighter Group** – P-47s Code letters: 509th Fighter Sqn 'G9-', 510th FS '2Z-', 511th FS 'K4-'
Afterwards:	Became Airspeed main factory and flight test site – de Havilland after 1951. Closed 1962. Now housing and industry

CHRISTCHURCH FOLLOWED the pattern of many south-east airfields, with the sudden influx of a D-Day support unit, using the ubiquitous P-47D, followed by a quick deployment to the Continent to continue to struggle. In the case of the 405th, it arrived in April and moved on to Picauville, France in June 1944.

CLUNTOE, Northern Ireland

Station:	238
Location:	South east of Cookstown, east of the B161, on the western shores of Lough Neath
Previously:	RAF – no flying. Transferred to USAAF Aug 1943
Major Units:	Combat Crew Replacement Center – 8th Composite Command
Afterwards:	Returned to RAF Nov 1944. Care and maintenance, June 1945. Briefly re-opened Feb 1953 to Feb 1955

WHEREAS ATCHAM (see earlier) dealt with preparing fighter pilots for the demanding conditions of the UK's airspace and climate, Cluntoe did the same for B-17 Fortress and, from February 1944, B-24 Liberator crews. Its USAAF period was brief, by the summer of 1944 the input had peaked and all US personnel had gone by November. Many traces of the airfield's wartime past are still evident.

National Cold War Exhibition

★ Within a landmark building at the RAF Museum Cosford, Shropshire, is the breathtaking National Cold War Exhibition which tells the story of the clash of ideologies via airframes, artefacts and stunning audiovisual displays. And of course there is much, more in the rest of the museum. 'Brown signed' from Junction 3 of the M54, open daily, times vary with the season. **More details on 01902 376200 or take a look at www.rafmuseum.org**

ABOVE LEFT: **Former DESERT THUNDER veteran, 20th Special Operations Squadron Sikorsky MH-53M PAVE LOW is displayed within the impressive National Cold War Exhibition.** KEN ELLIS

LEFT: **Cosford's General Dynamics F-111F 74-0177 served with the 492nd Fighter Squadron, part of the 48th Tactical Fighter Wing at Lakenheath.** KEY-STEVE FLETCHER

Paratroops checking their gear prior to embarking on a 37th Troop Carrier Squadron C-47 Skytrain at Cottesmore, June 1944. KEC
BELOW LEFT: On many runways in the UK, nose-to-tail assault gliders awaited their time to take part in Operation OVERLORD.
Horsas ready for the C-47s of the 316th Troop Carrier Group at Cottesmore. KEC

LEFT: A Waco CG-4 assault glider alongside C-47s of Cottesmore's 316th Troop Carrier Group. KEC

COTTESMORE, Leicestershire

Station:	489
Location:	North east of Oakham and of the village of Cottesmore
Previously:	RAF from Mar 1938, various use, mostly Bomber Command and OTU
Major Units:	Ninth Air Force, **316th Troop Carrier Group** – C-47s, C-53s and Waco CG-4s
	Code letters: 36th Troop Carrier Sqn '4C-', 37th TCS '6E-', 44th TCS 'T3-', 45th TCS 'W7-'
Afterwards:	Returned to the RAF Sep 1945. Varied use almost continuously since, including the Tornado Tri-National Training Establishment 1981 to 1999. Home to the RAF's front-line Harrier Force until the base closed in March 2012; it is now Kendrew Barracks.

ANOTHER EAST Midlands airfield used by the Ninth Air Force and its aerial armadas to liberate Europe. As an 'Expansion Period' base, Cottesmore's facilities were luxurious in comparison with the other Ninth airfields in the region and Troop Carrier Command set up its HQ here. The C-47s, C-53 and CG-4s of the 316th arrived in February 1944 and took part in OVERLORD and MARKET, among others. The 316th also operated a handful of C-46s and C-109s and left Cottesmore in May 1945.

Mighty Cottesmore is now an army camp; looking north east. KEY

An unidentified 493rd Bomb Group B-24 at Debach, 1944. Newly-applied armour plate below the cockpit has obliterated part of the nose-art, which most likely reads 'Mairzy Doats'. USAFA VIA WARREN E THOMPSON

DEBACH, Suffolk

Station	152
Location:	West of Wickham Market, south of the B1078
Previously:	Built for the USAAF, 1944
Major Units:	Eighth Air Force, **493rd Bomb Group** – B-24s, B-17s
	Group markings: Red band on tail, wings, tailplanes
	Code letters: 860th Bomb Sqn 'N6-', 861st BS 'Q4-', 862nd BS '8M-', 863rd BS 'G6-'
Afterwards:	Prisoner of war camp 1946, quickly returned to agriculture. Little remains of the airfield today.

PROBLEMS WITH the runway construction at Debach plagued the airfield's use. The 493rd flew B-24Hs and 'Js May 1944 to September 1944, changing to B-17Gs that month through to August 1945. Debach was home to the last Eighth Air Force Bomb Group to become operational; the 493rd making its debut on D-Day.

Centred on USAAF Station 152's former control tower, **493rd Bomb Group 'Helton's Hellcats' Museum** has been painstakingly put together. The website also includes a vast amount of material: for example, the locals pronounce it 'Deb-idge', while Americans call it 'Dee-bark'. Open the last Sunday of the month, April to September. More details at **www.493bgdebach.co.uk**

Protected by a sandbagged revetment, P-51D 'Jan' of the 4th Fighter Group's 334th Fighter Squadron at Debden, 1945. HENDEL COLLECTION VIA WARREN E THOMPSON

Captain Don S Gentile poses with his 4th Fighter Group, 336th Fighter Squadron P-51D at Debden. Born in Ohio to Italian immigrants, Gentile learned to fly at high school and enlisted in the RAF in September 1940. He joined 133 'Eagle' Squadron RAF at Debden in June 1942, transferring to the newly-established 4th Fighter Group in September. In March 1944 he claimed over half of his eventual total of 19.84 'kills': 7.5 Bf 109s, 3 Fw 190s and a Do 217.

BILL HESS VIA WARREN E THOMPSON

Debden, looking south – only one of the original hangars is intact. KEY

DEBDEN, Essex

Station:	356
Location:	South of Saffron Walden, north of the village
Previously:	Built 1937, ex RAF Sep 1942
Major Units:	Eighth Air Force, **4th Fighter Group** – Spitfires, P-47s, P-51s
	Code letters: 334th Fighter Sqn 'XR-' for Spitfires, 'QP-' for P-47s and P-51s, 335th FS 'AV-', then 'WD-', 336th FS 'MD-', then 'VF-'
Afterwards:	To RAF Sep 1945, varied usage to 1973. Now army barracks

IN MAY 1942 the RAF's 71 Squadron flew into Debden in its Spitfire Vs. One of three US-manned 'Eagle' squadrons within the RAF, Debden was to be the venue to amalgamate these within the USAAF. The 4th FG was formed from 71 Squadron (the 334th FS); 121 Squadron (335th FS) and 133 Squadron (336th FS). The 4th adopted P-47s from March 1943 and P-51s from February 1944. The USAAF vacated Debden in July 1945 when 'The Eagles' moved to Steeple Morden, Cambs.

DEENETHORPE, Northamptonshire

Station:	128
Location:	East of Corby and Weldon, between the A43 and the A427
Previously:	Built for the USAAF, 1943
Major Units:	Eighth Air Force, **401st Bomb Group** – B-17s
	Group markings: S in a triangle
	Code letters: 612th Bomb Sqn 'SC-', 613th BS 'IN-', 614th BS 'IW-', 615th BS 'IY-'
Afterwards:	To the RAF Jun 1945, but no flying use, closed 1946

EQUIPPED WITH B-17Gs, the 401st earned two Distinguished Unit Citations in over 7,000 missions. Among the 401st's many exploits were missions in support of OVERLORD, hitting Peenemünde in August 1944 and bombing for the Rhine Crossing. Today, a section of runway and part of the perimeter track are used by a thriving general aviation community.

Until 1996 it was possible to frame Deenethorpe's memorial to the 401st Bomb Group with the control tower – alas no more. KEN ELLIS

ABOVE: **With Corby in the background, Deenethorpe, looking west. Once B-17s thundered here, now it is home to light aircraft.** KEY

BELOW: **Construction work was always a hazard at airfields. Douglas-built B-17G 42-107009 of the 613th Bomb Squadron was caught out by drainage work at Deenethorpe in July 1944. Application of its nose-art, 'Lady Jane', is incomplete. This Fortress was declared missing in action on a raid to Hamburg on November 6, 1944. All nine crew survived, becoming prisoners of war.**
US NATIONAL ARCHIVES

DEOPHAM GREEN, Norfolk

Station:	142
Location:	West of the village of Deopham Green, itself west of Wymondham, between the B1108 and the A11
Previously:	Built for the USAAF, Feb 1944
Major Units:	Eighth Air Force, **452nd Bomb Group** – B-17s
	Group markings: L in a square
	Code letters: 728th Bomb Sqn 'M3-', 729th BS '9Z-',730th BS '7D-', 731st BS ('6K-'
Afterwards:	To the RAF for maintenance unit use Oct 1945, closed 1945, reverting to agriculture

B-17G FLYING Fortresses were not the dominant type in Norfolk, the 452nd being one of three bases (plus Fersfield and Watton to a minor extent) to be equipped with the type. Largely agricultural these days, there are plenty of traces of Station 142, if you know what to look for!

ABOVE: **B-17G 42-97069 'Mon Tete Rouge II' (My Red Head) of Deopham Green's 452nd Bomb Group, 731st Bomb Squadron, March 1944.** US NATIONAL ARCHIVES

RIGHT: **Simple but poignant: Deopham's memorial dedicated to all who served at Station 142.** KEY

FAR RIGHT: **Former B-17G base Deopham Green still bears traces of its past.** PETE WEST © 2013

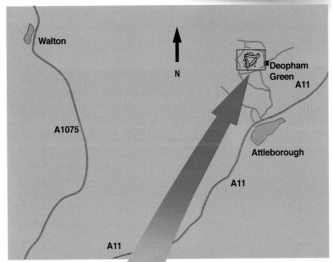

DUNKESWELL, Devon

Station:	173 – also US Navy facility 804
Location:	On minor roads north of Honiton, Devon
Previously:	US from operational, August 1942
Major Units:	479th Anti-Submarine Group (4th, 6th, 19th, 22nd Sqns) – B24Ds
	US Navy, Fleet Air Wing 7 (FAW-7), US Navy (VB-103, -105, -110) – PB4Y-1 Liberators
Afterwards:	To RAF Jul 1945, 16 Ferry Unit. Airfield sold off Feb 1949

THE USAAF's 479th Anti-Submarine Group moved in from St Eval, Cornwall, in August 1943 and flew sorties from the airfield until the US Navy took over in the form of FAW-7 from November 1943. The base did not formally become a navy facility until March 1944. FAW-7 was involved in the sinking of four U-boats during 1944-1945. The final U-boat 'kill' from Dunkeswell fell to a PBY-5A Catalina of VP-63 on detachment to the Devon base, in April 1945. Anti-submarine missions from Dunkeswell amounted to 62,247 flight hours. The airfield is a thriving light aviation centre; sadly the local museum closed early in 2012.

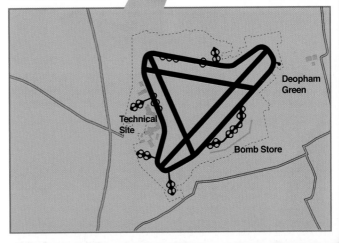

DUXFORD, Cambridgeshire

Station: 357
Location: At Junction 10 of the M11 (with the A505) west of Duxford village
Previously: RAF from Mar 1918. USAAF from Apr 1943
Major Units: Eighth Air Force, **78th Fighter Group** – P-47s and P-51s
Code letters: 82nd Fighter Sqn 'MX-', 83rd FS 'HL-', 84th FS 'WZ-'
Afterwards: To the RAF Aug 1945, flying ceased Jul 1961

DUXFORD'S ASSOCIATIONS with Americans go back to its World War One days when it hosted a variety of US units. From April 1943, it was home to the 78th FG operating P-47Cs and then P-51Ds, amassing 338 air 'kills'. The 78th left in August 1945 and the station reverted to the RAF for a further long and illustrious career until 1961. In 1968 the airfield provided part of the set for the *Battle of Britain* film and it was then that the abomination of destroying the middle of the three 'Belfast Truss' hangars was carried out, all for a mere movie. From the early 1970s, the airfield came alive again under the Imperial War Museum.

P-51B 'Ginger' of Duxford's 78th Fighter Group, 84th Fighter Squadron. PETE WEST © 2013

Lt Sumwatt and his ground crew pose with his 83rd Fighter Squadron P-47C Thunderbolt at Duxford, February 1944. US NATIONAL ARCHIVES

Work on its mighty Pratt & Whitney R-2800 complete, ground crew get ready to put the cowlings back on an 83rd Fighter Squadron P-47D at Duxford. US NATIONAL ARCHIVES

Tribute to American Air Power

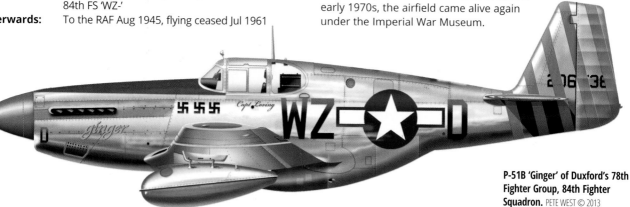

HM Queen Elizabeth II opened the £11m American Air Museum at Duxford on August 1, 1997 marking the culmination of many years of formulating, fund raising, preparing exhibits and constructing the landmark structure designed by Sir Norman Foster. Set on two levels, there are priceless moments when visitors suddenly grasp that among all the aircraft and supporting exhibits is a B-52 Stratofortress, its 185ft (56.38m) wingspan emphasizing the size of the building. Two walls on the lower floor carry the names of 28,000 airmen lost in action. Around the outside of the curved walls is another form of remembrance – 52 glass panels entitled 'Counting the Cost', conceived by sculptor Renato Niemis. These carry outlines of the 7,031 aircraft – fighters and bombers – lost in action during World War Two. **More details at www.eastessexaviationsociety.org**

Duxford's Flagship – 'Sally B'

Main image: 'Sally B' overflying the former B-17 base at Bassingbourn. Insets: On the starboard side, the B-17G carries the nose-art of the 91st Bomb Group's 'Memphis Belle' in honour of the starring role that 'Sally B' had in the 1990 movie. The port side carries the 'Sally B' nose-art. KEY-DUNCAN CUBITT

⭐ This year is the 38th flying season for a British treasure, Boeing B-17G Sally B – now Europe's last remaining airworthy Flying Fortress. Based at Duxford since March 1975, 'Sally B' is a flying memorial to the US airmen who gave their lives during the European war. Since 1982, 'Sally B' has been operated by Elly Sallingboe of B-17 Preservation Ltd with the help of a dedicated team of volunteers and the backing of one of the largest supporters clubs of its kind in the world – the 'Sally B' Supporters Club. Permanently based at the Imperial War Museum at Duxford, when not flying, 'Sally B' is on static display. The big bomber is not part of the museum's own collection and relies solely on charitable donations, sponsorship, sales of souvenirs, and the loyal support of her working team of volunteers as well as the 8,000 Supporters Club Members. Operating a large, four-engined aircraft is extremely expensive and the costs must be met if Sally B is to continue her mission. It is up to us all to keep their legacy alive – but 'Sally B' needs more support to continue to do so; to see how you can help take a look at: **www.sallyb.org.uk**

Duxford is well known as a haven for 'warbirds' including those of The Fighter Collection. On April 21, 2012 the latest restoration from the TFC workshops took to the air, Curtiss-built P-47G Thunderbolt 225068 'Snafu'. This carries the markings of the Duxford-based 78th Fighter Group's 84th Fighter Squadron. COL POPE

P-47D Thunderbolt of the 78th Fighter Group's, 82nd Fighter Squadron. KEY COLLECTION

Impressive memorial at the entrance to Earls Colne. KEN ELLIS

EARLS COLNE, Essex

Station:	358
Location:	South east of Halstead, south of the village
Previously:	USAAF from operational, May 1943
Major Units:	Ninth Air Force, **323rd Bomb Group** – B-26s
	Code letters: 453rd Bomb Sqn 'VT-', 454th BS 'RJ-', 455th BS 'YU-', 456th BS 'WT-'
Afterwards:	453rd to Beaulieu, Hants, Jul 1944. To RAF that month, airfield closed Jun 1946

EARLS COLNE briefly housed the 94th BG's B-17s May to June 1943. Today the site is part of a major leisure complex including a major golf club and a thriving general aviation operation.

Earls Colne is a tribute to how a former airfield can be used to the maximum, including aviation: the present-day grass strip follows the line of the western secondary runway. KEN ELLIS

EAST KIRKBY, Lincolnshire

Location:	South west of Spilsby, south of the village of east Kirkby and the A155
Previously:	RAF from Aug 1943, care and maintenance from Feb 1948
Major Units:	Strategic Air Command, 1958
Afterwards:	Returned to the RAF in 1959, no flying and airfield sold in 1970

AS LANCASTER *Just Jane* powers up and taxies in front of the famous control tower at East Kirkby few could believe as they look around them that the US had an influence on the airfield, let alone the post-war Strategic Air Command. The base was massively re-engineered 1955-1958 and was probably going to accept SAC fighters to defend bases and bombers. This never took place and today it is an atmospheric tribute to the valour of Bomber Command as the Lincolnshire Aviation Heritage Centre: 01790 763207 **www.lincsaviation.co.uk**

As the village sign proudly declares, East Kirkby was and is about the Lancaster. It was radically reshaped for Strategic Air Command, but was never used. KEN ELLIS

EAST WRETHAM, Norfolk

Station:	134
Location:	West of the A1075, west of Wretham
Previously:	RAF from Mar 1940, much operational usage
Major Units:	USAAF from Aug 1943
	Eighth Air Force, **359th Fighter Group** – P-47s and P-51s
	Code letters: 368th Fighter Sqn 'CV-', 369th FS 'IV-', 370th FS 'CR-' for the P-47s, 'CS-' for the P-51s
Afterwards:	To RAF Nov 1945. Airfield returned to agriculture by late 1954. Camp area (northern part of base) within major army training area

THE WORDS 'Danger Area' can be seen in stark red all over any road map of the Wretham area – this is the army's Stanford Training Area and a large chunk of the former fighter airfield lies within it. Those same maps show a minor road going west out of Wretham and it was to the south of this that the airfield lay, tracks going to the south marking its extent. The 359th's green cowled and spinnered P-47Ds, gave way to P-51Bs and 'Cs from April 1944, and from September 1944 to P-51Ds and even some 'Ks. The USAAF had gone by November 1945.

P-51D Mustang 44-14733 'Daddy's Girl' of East Wretham's 359th Fighter Group's 370th Fighter Squadron. PETE WEST © 2013

Firefly FR.1 MB726 of 814 Squadron overflying RNAS Eglinton, 1947. KEC

EGLINTON, Northern Ireland

Station:	344
Location:	North east of Londonderry, north of the A2 and the town of Eglinton
Previously:	RAF. Used by USAAF from Jul 1942
Major Units:	Eighth Air Force, **52nd Fighter Group**, 2nd, 4th and 5th Fighter Squadrons
Afterwards:	Returned to RAF Jan 1943 and to the Fleet Air Arm in May 1943

THE SPITFIRE Vs of the 52nd FG touched down at Eglinton in July 1942. Still in residence at that time was the similarly equipped RAF 152 Squadron and this unit helped the USAAF work up. In September, the 52nd vacated Station 344 for Goxhill, Lincs. The 82nd FG arrived the following month, using Spitfire Vs before its P-38s arrived in December and the unit moved to North Africa. Both the 52nd and the 82nd used nearby Maydown as a satellite. Today, the site thrives as Londonderry Airport.

EXETER, Devon

Station:	463
Location:	On the A30 east of the city, Devon
Previously:	Exeter Airport. RAF from Sep 1939. USAAF from Apr 1944
Major Units:	Ninth Air Force, **440th Troop Carrier Group** – C-47s and CG-4A Hadrians

	Code letters: 95th Troop Carrier Sqn '9X-', 96th TCS '6Z-', 97th TCS 'W6-', 98th TCS '8Y-'
Afterwards:	To RAF Sep 1944. Became Exeter Airport again in Jan 1947 and thriving as such

AS WITH many airfields used by the Ninth's Troop Carrier Command, Exeter followed an established – and hectic – pattern. After forming up at Bottesford, Leics, the 440th TCG moved into Exeter with C-47 Skytrains and Waco CG-4A Hadrians in readiness for D-Day. They took part of the US 101st Airborne Division into battle, followed up by constant re-supply flights. In September 1944 the 440th moved on, to Reims, in France.

EYE, Suffolk

Station:	134
Location:	North west of the village of Eye, close to the A140
Previously:	Built for the USAAF, handed over Feb 1944
Major Units:	Eighth Air Force, **490th Bomb Group** – B-24s and B-17s
	Group markings: T in a square
	Code letters: 848th Bomb Sqn '7W-', 849th BS 'W8-', 850th BS '7Q-', 851st BS 'S3-'
Afterwards:	Returned to agriculture late 1945; now light industry

ARRIVING IN April 1944, the 490th flew B-24s until August when it switched to B-17s. The last of 158 missions took place on April 20, 1945 and all had gone silent by August.

A B-52H at the end of a
very long-range mission
to Iraq at Fairford, 1991.
KEY–DUNCAN CUBITT

FAIRFORD, Gloucestershire

Location:	South of the A417, north of Swindon
Previously:	RAF from Jan 1944; to care and maintenance 1948, To USAF 1950
Major Units	See below

AN RAF station from March 1944 to December 1948, the base was massively regenerated for US Strategic Air Command. The first Convair B-36 Peacemakers arrived on detachment in February 1953 and later it was the Boeing B-47 Stratojet most often seen. The base reverted to RAF use in 1964 and famously became the test centre for Concordes 1969-1977. From 1978 Fairford again became a USAF asset with the temporary deployment of Boeing KC-135 Stratotankers in support of SAC operations. The KC-135s were involved in the raid on Libya in April 1986 and Fairford became a Boeing B-52 Stratofortress base for Operation DESERT STORM, 1990-1991 and again for Operation IRAQI FREEDOM, 2003. Fairford remains an active staging post for a variety of USAF operations.

An empty-looking Fairford in 1961 showing the size and complexity of the base. KEC

FERSFIELD, Norfolk

Station:	554
Location:	North of Fersfield Common, west of the B1077 between Winfarthing and Shelfanger
Previously:	Built for the USAAF, Mar 1944, operational from July 1944 – see below
Major Units:	See below
Afterwards:	Returned to RAF Nov 1944 – little if any usage. Airfield layout in the form of farm tracks still very evident

PACK 20,400lb (9,253kg) into a stripped out B-17, or 24,240lb (10,995kg) into a B-24, equip it with radio-controlled gear allowing it to be guided by a 'Mother' ship to a highly-protected but vital target and you have Project APHRODITE for the USAAF and ANVIL for the US Navy. To ease the technology, a volunteer, minimum crew would take the explosive-laden craft off, get them stabilised and on course, and then 'hit the silk'. The main 'clients' of these massive flying-bombs were to be V-weapon sites in France. In the middle of nowhere, Fersfield Common was an ideal place for such trials and USAAF Station 554 was born.

The base was operational from July 1944 with the first APHRODITE being trialled, unsuccessfully, on August 4, 1944. It was the first of 18 utilising B-17Fs and 'Gs. The 388th Bomb Group from Knettishall, Suffolk, was placed in charge of running the USAAF project, with its 560th Bomb Squadron being deputed. The US Navy's Special Air Unit 1 was established to run ANVIL, itself a sub-unit of the US Navy Station at Dunkeswell, Devon. As well as the APHRODITE – ANVIL missions, Fersfield was also used for Project BATTY, experimenting with GB-4 TV-guided bombs.

On August 12, 1944, the one and only US Navy ANVIL flight took off, with Lockheed PV-1 Venturas acting as 'Mothers'. Close to Blythburgh, Suffolk, the 24,240lb of TNT inside PB4Y-1 Liberator 32271 ignited, virtually vaporising the aircraft and certainly its crew: Lts J P Kennedy and W J Willy. Kennedy was son of Joseph, then US Ambassador to London, and brother to John Fitzgerald, destined to be the 35th President of the USA in 1960. Trials of APHRODITE (and its improved CASTOR variant) and BATTY bombs moved to Knettishall in November 1944 for further testing. Fersfield fell back into agriculture and quiet.

P-51D 'Tar Heel' of the 339th Fighter's Group's 505th Fighter Squadron at Fowlmere, early **1945.** JOHN FRANZ VIA WARREN E THOMPSON

Many Troop Carrier Groups would also be equipped with Waco CG-4 Hadrian assault gliders, which would be towed into battle behind C-47s. US NATIONAL ARCHIVES

FOLKINGHAM, Lincolnshire

Station:	489
Location:	South east of Grantham, west of Aslackby and the A15
Previously:	Handed over on completion to the USAAF
Major Units:	Ninth Air Force, **313th Troop Carrier Group** – C-47s, C-53s and Waco CG-4s
	Code letters: 29th Troop Carrier Sqn '5X-', 47th TCS 'N3-', 48th TCS 'Z7-', 49th TCS 'H2-'
Afterwards:	To the RAF Mar 1945, non-flying use then care and maintenance. Thor missile site 1959-1963. Site sold off 1964 and very little evident today

LIKE MANY other airfields used for airborne operations across the country, Folkingham saw only a short operational life, but that was intense. Arriving in February 1944, the 313th was involved in OVERLORD and the ops through to Arnhem and beyond. As well as the 'standard' C-47, C-53, CG-4 'mix', the 313th also operated a few C-46s and even trialled the large Waco CG-13 assault glider.

FORD, Sussex

Station:	362
Location:	East of Yapton and the B2233, south west of Ford
Previously:	RFC/RAF from 1918 – see below. Closed 1920. Civil from 1931, FAA from 1939, then RAF, then FAA
Major Units:	See below
Afterwards:	Closed as FAA base 1958, much of site becoming a prison

DURING ITS World War One era, Ford was briefly home to the US 92nd Aero Squadron with a variety of bomber types, including Farman F.40s. The Americans stayed until November 1918. Ford had a very busy and crowded World War Two operational history and in amongst this it was allocated to the Eighth Air Force as a forward base for fighter units from July 1943 until mid-1944.

FOWLMERE, Cambridgeshire

Station:	378
Location:	South west of the village, west of the B1368
Previously:	RAF from Mar 1940. To USAAF Mar 1944
Major Units:	Eighth Air Force, **339th Fighter Group** – P-51s
	Code letters: 503rd Fighter Sqn 'D7-', 504th FS '5Q-', 505th FS '6N-'
Afterwards:	To the RAF Oct 1945, flying ceased 1946.

IN 1918 there was an extensive military airfield at Fowlmere with US units in residence, but it was not on the site of the World War Two airfield and was cleared in the early 1920s. The airfield began life in 1940 as a satellite of Duxford and was home to a variety of units. The 339th FG arrived in March 1944 with P-51Bs, later adopting 'Cs, 'Ds and 'Ks. The Ministry of Defence sold off the airfield in the early 1950s. From 1986 it was reborn as a general aviation airfield and it continues to thrive, sometimes in its former role as a 'satellite' for Duxford, taking light aircraft visitors bound for major airshows down the road.

FRAMLINGHAM, Suffolk

Station:	153
Location:	On the B1116 north of Woodbridge, east of the village of Parham – airfield also known at Parham
Previously:	Built for the USAAF, 1943
Major Units:	Eighth Air Force, **390th Bomb Group**, 'Wittan's Wallopers' – B-17s Group markings: J in a square Code letters: 568th Bomb Sqn 'BI-', 569th BS 'CC-', 570th BS 'DI-', 571st BS 'FC-'
Afterwards:	To the RAF Aug 1945 as storage site. One hangar retained for storage by MoD. Small airstrip still used on the site and home to the Parham Airfield Museum

Part of the extensive displays at the Parham Airfield Museum. KEY-KEN ELLIS

DURING MAY and June 1943 the B-17Fs of the 95th Bomb Group operated from Framlingham before 'Wittan's Wallopers', the 390th BG, moved in with its B-17Gs. The unit went on to complete 320 missions and the gallantry of its personnel is shown off amid many other exhibits inside the excellent former control tower and other buildings that form the Parham Airfield Museum.

The tower houses the superb **Parham Airfield Museum**, which incorporates the 390th Bomb Group Memorial Air Museum and the Museum of British Resistance. The latter is dedicated to the work of the Auxiliary Units – the so-called 'Stay Behind' cells in the event of an invasion. 'Brown signed' from the A12, open Sundays and Bank Holidays, April to October and extended times in the summer. 01728 621373 **www.parhamairfield museum.co.uk**

FULBECK, Lincolnshire

Station:	488
Location:	East of Newark, south of the A17, near Stragglethorpe
Previously:	RAF from Jun 1940, used for training and later assault glider storage
Major Units:	Ninth Air Force, **434th Troop Carrier Group** – C-47s, C-53s, Airspeed Horsas and Waco CG-4s Code letters: 71st Troop Carrier Sqn 'CJ-', 72nd TCS 'CU-', 74th TCS 'IN-' Ninth AAF, **442nd Troop Carrier Group** – C-47s Code letters: 303rd Troop Carrier Sqn 'J7-', 304th TCS 'V4-', 305th TCS '4J-', 306th TCS '7H-'
Afterwards:	Returned to the RAF Jul 1944, used by Bomber Command and then as a satellite to Cranwell, later for storage and exercises. Closed 1973, although elements still with MoD

THE 434TH TCG flew C-47s and C-53s and towed CG-4s and Airspeed Horsas and moved on to Aldermaston, Berks, for further operations in January 1944. The 442nd arrived in March 1944 and flew to the D-Day drop zones undertaking re-supply missions before moving on to Weston Zoyland, Somerset in July 1944.

View from, and of, the restored tower at Framlingham, once the home of 'Wittan's Wallopers'. KEY-KEN ELLIS

Members of the US Army's 809th Aviation Engineering Battalion laying the runways at Glatton, 1943. KEC

View from the tower at Glatton showing the signals square and the 'GT' airfield denominator. US NATIONAL ARCHIVES

Now known as Peterborough Conington, Glatton's east-west runway still serves local light aviation. KEN ELLIS

Just as at RAF stations, British Air Training Corps cadets were made welcome at USAAF bases: John Wilson with personnel of Glatton's 749th Bomb Squadron, March 1945. KEC

GLATTON, Cambridgeshire

Station:	130
Location:	South of the B660, east of the A1M, south east of Stilton
Previously:	Built for the USAAF, 1943
Major Units:	Eighth Air Force, **457th Bomb Group** – B-17s
	Group markings: U in a triangle
	Squadron colours: 748th Bomb Sqn with red prop centres, 749th BS blue, 750th BS white, 751st BS yellow
Afterwards:	To the RAF Jul 1945 briefly a satellite of Upwood, care and maintenance April 1946 and sold off in 1948. Currently Peterborough Business Aerodrome, general aviation

TURNING FINALS on Runway 28, the London to Edinburgh railway line runs north-south, float over the Holme to Conington road – previously the perimeter track – down onto the numbers and luxuriate that where today a thriving light aircraft population touched down, so did countless B-17 sorties during World War Two. Today this is Peterborough Business Aerodrome, or Conington, but during the war it was known as Glatton, a village immediately to the west and severed from the airfield by the A1M Great North Road. The airfield was the sole preserve of the 457th BG, January 1944 to June 1945, a unit that shunned unit identification codes and opted for colour-coded propeller centres instead. The 457th had a valiant, if costly, war – over 80 B-17s were lost in action in just over 7,000 sorties.

Glatton's imposing memorial. NIGEL PRICE

At Work

A posed image of engine maintenance on an 'Invasion'-striped P-51.
US NATIONAL ARCHIVES

Armourers readying ammunition belts for a P-61 Black Widow, probably at **Hurn.** US NATIONAL ARCHIVES

Without mechanics, medics and a barrage of other specialists, a base could not function. These images pay tribute to 'those who also serve'

Armourers checking out a 0.5-cal machine-gun before it is fitted to a P-51 of the 436th Fighter Squadron at Wattisham. KEC

A British seamstress acting as a volunteer with Wattisham's 'Red Cross Club' applying the famous 'Mighty Eighth' patch for a publicity shot. KEC

Sentry duty need not be strenuous! Keeping watch from a pillbox on Wattisham's perimeter. KEC

Wattisham's photo-lab and its crew. KEC

Ground crew with a 479th Fighter Group Mustang at Wattisham. KEC

Recycling of all usable spares was vital to ease the burdens of the transatlantic supply convoys. Stripping down a B-17, probably at one of the massive Base Air Depots. US NATIONAL ARCHIVES

GOSFIELD, Essex

Station:	154
Location:	West of Halstead, north west of the village
Previously:	USAAF from operational, Dec 1943
Major Units:	Ninth Air Force, **365th Fighter Group** – P-47s
	Code letters: 386th Fighter Sqn 'D5-', 387th FS 'B4-',
	388th FS 'C4-'
	Ninth Air Force, **410th Bomb Group** – A-20s
	Code letters: 644th Bomb Sqn '5D-', 645th BS '7X-',
	646th BS '8U-', 647th BS '6Q-'
Afterwards:	To RAF Sep 1944. Airfield closed late 1945

P-47s PROVIDING cover for Ninth Air Force B-26s were the first residents at Gosfield, from December 1943. The 365th FG moved to Beaulieu, Hants, in March 1944. Next was the 410th BG which had spent just 12 days at Birch (see above) before settling here with its Douglas A-20 Havocs. It used the A-20s tactically, often in large formations until moving to Coulommiers, France, in September 1944. Today, little remains of the former airfield.

GOXHILL, Lincolnshire

Station:	345
Location:	East of Barton-upon-Humber and of Goxhill village
Previously:	RAF, Bomber Command, from June 1941
Major Units:	Eighth Air Force, **496th Fighter Training Group**,
	554th Fighter Sqn 'B9-', Dec 1943 to Aug 1944;
	555th Fighter Sqn 'C7-', Dec 1943 to Feb 1945
Afterwards:	Returned to the RAF Mar 1945, used as a storage site. Much of the base remains

A-20 Havoc of Gosfield's 645th Bomb Squadron. US NATIONAL ARCHIVES

Close formation of 410th Bomb Group, 646th BS A-20 Havocs. US NATIONAL ARCHIVES

Gosfield-based
Havocs at low
level over a
much-repaired
enemy airfield.
US NATIONAL ARCHIVES

WHILE GOXHILL was off the beaten track for a USAAF base, like Atcham in Shropshire it was ideal to act as a fighter introduction centre. From June 1942 a series of units came through to get used to the UK's crowded airspace and, of course, the weather! Longest 'tenant' was the 78th FG which arrived in December 1942 and moved to Duxford, Cambs, in April 1943. The Fighter Training Group channelled new pilots into units needing replacements. The 554th flew Lockheed P-38H and 'J Lightnings, and the 555th North American P-51B and 'C Mustangs. The 496th moved to Halesworth, Suffolk, in February 1945.

LEFT: **Goxhill, looking south-west. Extraction of hardcore from the runways for road building has resulted in several ponds.** KEY

BELOW: **Spitfire Vb W3815 of the 496th Fighter Training Group's 555th Fighter Squadron at Goxhill, early 1944.**
PETER GREEN COLLECTION

'Boss Lady', B-17G 42-97271 of the 384th Bomb Group's 545th Bomb Squadron. The 545th's unit codes were 'JD-', but many 545th aircraft, separated the letters on the port side. PETE WEST © 2013

GRAFTON UNDERWOOD, Northamptonshire

Station:	106
Location:	East of Kettering, north of the village of Grafton Underwood
Previously:	RAF from Oct 1941. To USAAF May 1942
Major Units:	Eighth Air Force, **97th Bomb Group**, 340th, 341st, 342nd, 414th Bomb Sqns – B-17s
	Eighth Air Force, **384th Bomb Group** – B-17s
	Group markings: P in a triangle
	Code letters: 544th Bomb Sqn 'SU-', 545th BS 'JD-', 546th BS 'BK-', 547th BS 'SO-'
Afterwards:	Returned to RAF Jun 1945, used for storage. Sold off 1959. Some traces of the base still to be found

"The first and last bombs dropped by the Eighth Air Force were from airplanes flying from Grafton Underwood" – one side of Station 106's memorial. KEN ELLIS

IT WAS from the runways at Grafton Underwood that the Fortress became a weapon of war with the USAAF when the 97th BG's B-17Es took off on August 17, 1942, for a railway hub near Rouen, France. The first B-17Fs arrived and the 97th moved to North Africa to join the 12th Air Force the following month. Next unit was the 384th, equipped with B-17Fs and later B-17Gs, and it went on to achieve 9,348 missions. In June 1945 it moved to Istres, France, for personnel transport duties.

GREAT ASHFIELD, Suffolk

Station:	155
Location:	North east of Elmswell, south of the village of Great Ashfield
Previously:	RAF Mar to Jun 1943. To the USAAF Jun 1943
Major Units:	Eighth Air Force, **385th Bomb Group**, 'Van's Valiants' – B-17s
	Group markings: G in a square
	Code letters: 548th Bomb Sqn 'GX-', 549th BS 'XA-', 550th BS 'SG-', 551st BS 'HR-'
Afterwards:	To RAF Jul 1945, closed Mar 1956. Sold off in 1962. Traces of the runway and other elements still to be seen

LIKE MANY bases, Great Ashfield was home only to one Bomb Group for its entire time as a USAAF base – June 1943 to June 1945. 'Van's Valiants', as the 385th was known, gained two Distinguished Unit Citations during its 296 missions and flew B-17Fs and then 'Gs.

GREAT DUNMOW, Essex

Station:	164
Location:	West of the village, north of the A120 – also known as Great Easton
Previously:	USAAF from operational, Sep 1943
Major Units:	Ninth Air Force, **386th Bomb Group** – B-26s
	Code letters: 552nd Bomb Sqn 'RG-', 553rd BS 'AN-', 554th BS 'RU-', 555th BS 'YA-'
Afterwards:	386th to Beaumont-sur-Oise, France, Oct 1944. To RAF Oct 1944, flying ceased Dec 1945. USAF storage site 1954-1958. Little remains of airfield.

B-26B 131624 'Loretta Young' of the 386th Bomb Group's 555th Bomb Squadron, Great Dunmow, mid-1944. © PETE WEST 2013

GREAT SAMPFORD, Essex

Station:	359
Location:	South east of Saffron Walden, west of the village
Previously:	RAF from April 1942
Major Units:	Eighth Air Force, **4th Fighter Group** (see under Debden) used it as a satellite and emergency landing ground until early 1944
Afterwards:	To RAF, non-flying, from Jun 1943. Sold off Mar 1946

GREENCASTLE, Northern Ireland

Station:	237
Location:	South west of Kilkeel, on the Cranfield Point peninsula
Previously:	RAF. Transferred to USAAF Sep 1943
Major Units:	Eighth Air Force, 4th Gunnery and Tow Target Squadron
Afterwards:	Returned to RAF May 1945

GREENCASTLE OPERATED in two very different ways. It was a Combat Crew Replacement Center but in the ground training role only, getting large numbers of air gunners ready for flying training at the CCRC at Greencastle. Providing something to aim at was the 4th G&TTS, flying A-20 Havocs and Vultee A-35 Vengeances. The base also acted as a satellite to 3rd BAD at Langford Lodge, taking large numbers of four-engined types for short-term storage. Much of the airfield's structure can still be seen.

RIGHT: **The World War Two layout of Greenham Common was obliterated in the creation of the sprawling Strategic Air Command base. Looking west from Crookham Common, 2002.** KEY

BELOW: **Lined up ready for a drop, C-47s at Greenham Common. 'Lilly Bell II' in the foreground belongs to the 89th Troop Carrier Squadron.** KEC

GREENHAM COMMON, Berkshire

Station:	486
Location:	South east of Newbury, north of the A339
Previously:	USAAF from operational, Sep 1942
Major Units:	Twelfth Air Force, **51st Troop Carrier Group**, Sep 1942 to Nov 1942
	Ninth Air Force, **438th Troop Carrier Group** – C-47s and CG-4As
	Code letters: 87th Troop Carrier Sqn '3X-', 88th TCS 'M2-', 89th TCS '4U-', 90th TCS 'Q7-'
Afterwards:	To RAF, non-flying and closed June 1946. See below for USAF use

HOSTING THE 51st TCW while it worked up to move to North Africa in November 1942, Greenham Common temporarily became an RAF training station April to October 1943. The C-47 and CG-4A equipped 438th TCW was heavily involved in all airborne operations from D-Day onwards and moved to France in February 1945. Greenham became a USAF base in mid-1951 and was massively expanded. It was used for Strategic Air Command Boeing B-47 Stratojet deployments under the REFLEX system from September 1953. B-47 deployments continued to 1964 with the base then taking on a variety of flying and non-flying roles. From May 1983 Greenham was in the headlines as a cruise missile base and it gained a new form of 'gate guardian' – a peace camp! Today the base is an extensive industrial estate.

'Wolfpack' P-47Cs and 'Ds of the 62nd Fighter Squadron on a sortie out of Halesworth. In the left foreground is Captain Eugene O'Neill's P-47C 41-6347 'Lil Abner'.
US NATIONAL ARCHIVES

GROVE, Berkshire

Station:	519
Location:	North west of Wantage, west of the village, Berks
Previously:	RAF from operational from Aug 1942
Major Units:	See below
Afterwards:	To RAF Feb 1946 – non-flying

GROVE WAS used by the USAAF as a support base with C-47s/C-53s and even Curtiss C-46 Commandos being maintained there. A large communications flight, using as variety of types, was also based. By late 1943 it was an extensive, and complex, storage base. Today, there is a technology park on the western perimeter, with an impressively-mounted DH Venom FB.54 as 'gate guardian'.

HALESWORTH, Suffolk

Station:	365
Location:	North east of Halesworth, east of the A144 – also known as Holton
Previously:	Built for the USAAF, 1943
Major Units:	Eighth Air Force, **56th Fighter Group** 'The Wolfpack' – P-47s Code letters: 61st Fighter Sqn 'HV-', 62nd FS 'LM-', 63rd FS 'UN-' Eighth Air Force, **489th Bomb Group** – B-24s Group markings: W in a circle Code letters: 844th Bomb Sqn, '4R-', 845th BS 'T4-', 846th BS '8R-', 847th BS 'S4-' Eighth Air Force 5th Emergency Rescue Sqn – see below for types operated 496th Fighter Training Croup – P-51Ds, Feb-Jun 1945

Afterwards:	To the RAF Aug 1945 and then briefly to the Fleet Air Arm. Returned to agriculture 1949. The road from Upper Holton north to Back's Green uses the south-west element of the perimeter track

NOW COVERED by an extensive turkey farm operated by a well-known company, Halesworth can boast varied usage by the USAAF. 'Hub' Zemke led the famous 56th FG 'Wolfpack' at the beginning and the end of its sojourn at Halesworth (May 1943 to April 1944). The 489th Bomb Group was resident for only seven months (May to November 1944) before becoming the first Eighth Air Force unit to be called home. The 5th Emergency Rescue Squadron operated Consolidated OA-10A Catalina amphibians, P-47Ds and a handful of airborne lifeboat-equipped B-17Gs for air-sea rescue – January to May 1945.

The **Halesworth Airfield Memorial Museum** and the **56th Fighter Group Museum** are well worth a visit. Open April to October, Sundays and Bank Holidays. More details:
www.halesworthairfield museum.org.uk

The Duxford-based Catalina operated by Plane Sailing Ltd flies in the colours of 'Miss Pick Up', and OA-10A flown by Halesworth's 5th Emergency Rescue Squadron. KEY-STEVE FLETCHER

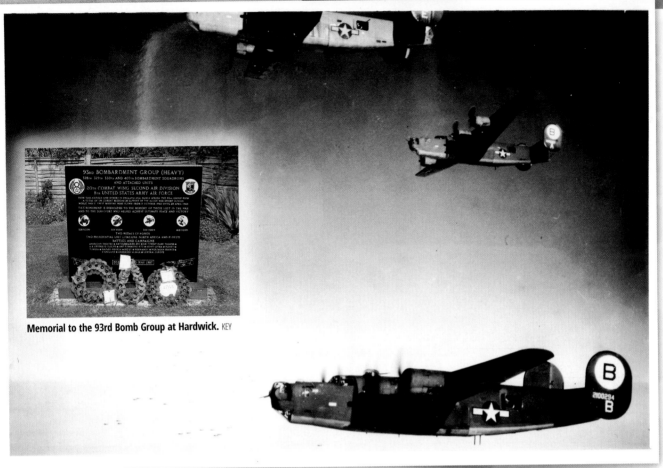

Memorial to the 93rd Bomb Group at Hardwick. KEY

B-24s of the 93rd Bomb Group. The aircraft at the bottom is 'Victory Belle', 42-100294 of the 328th Bomb Squadron. US NATIONAL ARCHIVES

HARDWICK, Norfolk

Station: 104
Location: East of Bungay, south west of the village of Topcroft Street. Hardwick itself is to the west of the airfield
Previously: Built for the USAAF Sep 1942
Major Units: Eighth Air Force, **93rd Bomb Group** – B-24s
Group markings: B in a circle
Code letters: 328th Bomb Sqn 'GO-', 329th BS 'RE-', 330th BS 'AG-', 409th BS 'YM-'
Afterwards: To RAF Jun 1945, airfield sold off in mid-1960s – see also below

THE B-24Ds of the 93rd arrived in December 1942 and were to establish no less than 396 operations – the largest in the Eighth Air Force. Of these 49 were from bases in North Africa in a series of deployments, which were to give rise to the unit's name 'Ted's Travelling Circus'. The 93rd's most famous deployment was in August 1943 for the incredible raid on the Ploesti oil fields in Romania. During this raid the 93rd took a mauling and earned a Distinguished Unit Citation in the process. From September 1943 the B-24Ds gave way to B-24Hs and 'Js. The 93rd left Hardwick in June 1945.

The **93rd Bomb Group Museum** is set in three Nissen huts on the former Station 104's Communal Site A, and is exceptional. Open the third Sunday of each month, May to October. Take a look at **www.93rd-bg-museum.org.uk**

B-24H 41-24226 'Joisey Bounce' in the foreground of an early operational formation of the 93rd Bomb Group, spring 1943. US NATIONAL ARCHIVES VIA WARREN E THOMPSON

HARRINGTON, Northamptonshire

Station:	179
Location:	South west of Rothwell, south of the A14 and Harrington village
Previously:	RAF from Nov 1943, bomber OTU
Major Units:	Eighth Air Force, **801st Bomb Group** – B-24s, C-47s, A-26Bs, Mosquitos 36th BS, 406th BS, 788th BS, 850th BS (renumbered as 856th, 858th, 859th and 857th respectively in Aug 1944 under the 'banner' of the 492nd BG), Mar 1944 to Dec 1945
Afterwards:	Returned to RAF 1945, no flying. Thor ICBM site 1959 to 1963, then to agriculture. Large amount of the airfield still recognisable

Cuban cigar deployed, Colonel J L Laughlin, CO of Headcorn's 362nd Fighter Group, in his P-47, 1944. VIA WARREN THOMPSON

Centred upon the hardened group operations building of what was once USAAF Station 179 and home of the clandestine 492nd and 801st Bomb Groups is the **'Carpetbagger' Aviation Museum**. Restored to its wartime state, it houses exhibitions describing the covert operations carried out by the US from Harrington and by the RAF from Tempsford, Bedfordshire. Open from Easter to October at weekends and Bank Holidays. More details: 01604 686608 **www.harringtonmuseum.org.uk**

The memorial at Harrington uses the famous image of an all-black Liberator taking off. KEN ELLIS

HARRINGTON WAS the main home of the famous 'Carpetbaggers', a unit designed to supply Special Operations Executive agents in the field and to 'deliver' them. Prime equipment was the B-24 (using 'D, 'H and 'J) but C-47s, DH Mosquito XVIs and Douglas A-26B Invaders were also used. The C-47s landed in occupied territory. Agent-dropping and supply operations were largely over by September 1944 and the 801st was then employed on a wide variety of other tasks, some mundane like fuel supply, others of a far more 'black' nature presaging the advent of the 'Cold War'.

HEADCORN, Kent

Station	412
Location:	West of Egerton Forstal, north west of Headcorn, Kent
Previously:	RAF Advanced Landing Ground from Jun 1943
Major Units:	Ninth Air Force, **362nd Fighter Group** – P-47s Code letters: 377th Fighter Sqn 'E4-', 378th 'G8-', 379th 'B8-'
Afterwards:	Site returned to agriculture Sep 1944

A MEMORIAL to the RCAF units that used the ALG during its RAF phase can be found on site. After D-Day the 362nd moved on to Lignerolles, France. Please note: the present-day Headcorn aerodrome was Lashenden Advanced Landing Ground during 1944 – see later.

Ford-built B-24H 42-51211 of the Harrington-based 'Carpetbaggers'.

Displayed inside 'Milestones of Flight' at Hendon is P-51D Mustang '413317' 'The Duck', donated by Bob Tullius of Florida. KEN ELLIS

HENDON, Greater London

Location: North-west London
Previously: Aerodrome from 1911
Major Units: See below
Afterwards: RAF station throughout World War Two. Home of the RAF Museum, from November 1972

The USAAF's Air Transport Command based C-47 Skytrains at Hendon and used them for communications work across the UK during late 1943 to October 1944.

Within the **Royal Air Force Museum** can be found many insights into USAAF and USAF history. Signposted from the end of the M1 and A41, it is open daily – check for details of seasonal variations. 020 8205 2266 **www.rafmuseum.org**

HESTON, Greater London

Station 510
Location: North east of London Heathrow Airport, north of the A4
Previously: Municipal airport from 1929
Major Units: See below
Afterwards: RAF use throughout World War Two. Closed by 1947

THE USAAF used Heston extensively as a communications airfield, its proximity to central London being a boon. The 27th Air Transport Group, operating a wide variety of types was resident from May 1943 as were several lesser units. The USAAF vacated the airfield in October 1944.

The role of the 'Mighty Eighth' is honoured at the RAF Museum Hendon in the Bomber Command Hall with B-17G 44-83868 in the colours of the Bury St Edmunds-based 94th Bomb Group. KEN ELLIS

SUBSCRIBE & SAVE

TO YOUR FAVOURITE MAGAZINE TODAY...

WIN LIMITED EDITION SWORDFISH 'CHANNEL DASH' PRINTS

*CLOSING DATE: JUNE 6, 2013

Britain's Top-Selling Aviation Monthly

FlyPast

Warbird Flight
Spectacular salute by Duxford fighters
PRESERVATION

FOR VALOUR
VC for a brave Hampden gunner
AIRCREW

B-52 OVER VIETNAM
Stratofortress in combat COLD WAR

Spotlight
Fairey Swordfish
Torpedo-carrying biplane in action
HISTORY

MEN BEHIND THE MEDALS WORLD WAR 2
'Twinkle' Pearson - a fearless Blenheim pilot

FORK-TAILED DEVIL WARBIRDS
Californian P-38 Lightning in detail

THE WHOLE SHOW VETERANS
The remarkable life of a long-serving pilot

APRIL 2013   £4.25   CAN $9.75   04>

9 770262 695214

www.flypast.com

Toppling A Giant

FlyPast is internationally regarded as the magazine for aviation history and heritage. Having pioneered coverage of this fascinating world of 'living history' since 1980, FlyPast still leads the field today. Each issue is packed with news and features on warbird preservation and restoration, museums, and the airshow scene. Subjects regularly profiled include British and American aircraft type histories, as well as those of squadrons and units from World War One to the Cold War.

Honey Bunny's LEGACY
ALLIED FIGHTERS' EXCEPTIONAL P-38 HAS A LONG AND INTRIGUING HISTORY, WHICH MICHAEL O'LEARY UNFOLDS

FlyPast LANCASTER
FlyPast Vulcan Swansong
FlyPast Maltese Falcon
FlyPast MOSQUITO AIRBORNE

Download on iTunes

ANDROID APP ON Google play

also available for PC, MAC & Kindle Fire from pocketmags.com

Available on the App Store

Search: FlyPast

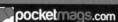

FREE APP with sample issue.
IN APP ISSUES £3.99

NEW: LORD ASHCROFT'S "HERO OF THE MONTH"

A HISTORY OF CONFLICT

BRITAIN AT WAR

BRITAIN'S BEST SELLING MILITARY HISTORY MONTHLY

LEADING SEAMAN JAMES MAGENNIS VC

SUICIDAL VALOUR
The King's former bodyguard in wartime 'mission impossible'

GIANT KILLERS
Battling the Axis transport aircraft

PLUS:

HMS AUDACIOUS: MINED 1914

Issue 71 MARCH 2013 £4.20

THE KING'S VISIT TO THE D-DAY BEACHES

FREE JETLINERS POSTER INSIDE

AVIATION NEWS

THE PAST, PRESENT AND FUTURE OF FLIGHT *Incorporating* Classic Aircraft

BOEING 737
10,500 Orders And Counting...

Mildenhall Air Fete
Airshow Flashback

EXCLUSIVE
A330 to the North Pole
Adventure by Air

Lightnings over Germany
Wideroe - Norway
Northern Pioneer

Spitfire Warpaint
Camouflaging a Classic

Super Hercules
The New Generation

MARCH 2013 £4.10

157/13

BRITAIN AT WAR is dedicated to exploring every aspect of Britain's involvement in conflicts from the turn of the 20th century through to modern day. From World War I to the Falklands, World War II to Iraq, readers are able to re-live decisive moments in Britain's history through fascinating insight combined with rare and previously unseen photography.

As Britain's longest established monthly aviation journal, **AVIATION NEWS** is renowned for providing the best coverage of every branch of aviation. Now incorporating Classic Aircraft magazine, each issue features latest news and in-depth features, plus firsthand accounts from pilots putting you in the cockpit. Covering both modern military and civil aircraft as well as classic types from yesteryear, Aviation News covers subjects from World War Two, through the Cold War years to present day.

 www.britainatwar.com

 www.aviation-news.co.uk

Available on the **App Store**

also available for PC, MAC & Kindle Fire from **pocketmags**.com

Download on **iTunes**

ANDROID APP ON **Google play**

Search:
Britain at War

Search:
Aviation news

FREE APP with sample issue.
IN APP ISSUES £3.99

KEY

EUROPE'S LEADING AVIATION PUBLISHER

FOR THE LATEST SUBSCRIPTION DEALS

 VISIT:
www.keypublishing.com/shop

 PHONE:
(UK) 01780 480404 (Overseas) +44 1780 480404

The displays at Hethel paid tribute not just to Station 114 but to Attlebridge as well. KEY-KEN ELLIS

HETHEL, Norfolk

Station	114
Location:	East of Wymondham, between the A11 and B1135, west of the village of Hethel
Previously:	Built for the USAAF, Nov 1942
Major Units:	Eighth Air Force, **389th Bomb Group** 'The Sky Scorpions' – B-24s Group markings: C in a circle Code letters: 564th Bomb Sqn 'YO-', 565th BS 'EE-', 566th BS 'RR-', 567th BS 'HP-'
Afterwards:	To the RAF Jun 1945 and used by a series of fighter units until placed into care and maintenance 1947.

THE 389th Bomb Group, 'The Sky Scorpions', received a Distinguished Unit Citation for its operations against Ploesti from North Africa in August 1943. The B-24Ds were replaced by B-24Hs, 'Js and later 'Ls and 'Ms from October 1943. The last mission was staged in April 1945 and by June the USAAF had gone. From 1964 Hethel earned other fame as the home of the sports car manufacturer Lotus.

Hethel is the venue for the combined **389th Bomb Group Memorial Exhibition** and **Home for the 466th BG Attlebridge**. The wartime chapel and the buildings around it provide a unique element of Eighth Air Force history. Open the second Sunday of the month, April to October. More: 01953 607147 **www.hethel389th.wordpress.com**

HIGH ERCALL, Shropshire

Station:	346
Location:	North of the B5062 between High Ercall and Crudgington
Previously:	RAF, 29 Maintenance Unit (MU). Occupied by USAAF Jun 1942
Major Units:	Eighth Air Force: 31st **Fighter Group** – 309th Fighter Squadron, **81st Fighter Group** – 92nd Fighter Squadron
Afterwards:	Returned to RAF Apr 1943

USED FROM late 1940 until February 1964 by 29 MU, the airfield became Station 346 for a brief period when it acted as a satellite for Atcham with the MU still functioning throughout. Equipped with Spitfire Vs, the 390th FS of the 31st FG used High Ercall from June to August 1942. Very brief use by P-38s of the 1st FG was followed by the Bell P-39 Airacobras of the 92nd FS from October to December. The airfield is in a good state of preservation.

HIGH HALDON, Kent

Station:	411
Location:	North of Tenterden, north of the A28, Kent
Previously:	RAF Advanced Landing Group from mid-1943 – no usage
Major Units:	Eighth Air Force, **358th Fighter Group** – P-47Ds Code letters: 365th Fighter Sqn 'CH-', 366th FS 'IA-', 367th FS 'CP-'
Afterwards:	RAF from Aug 1944, to farmland Sep 1944

THE THUNDERBOLTS of the 358th moved into the Advanced Landing Ground from Raydon, Suffolk, ready for D-Day. Brief RAF use was as an advanced base for 616 (South Yorkshire) Squadron's Gloster Meteor Is on their anti-V-1 sorties.

Spitfire Vb BM635 of the 31st Fighter Group, 309th Fighter Squadron at High Ercall, June 1942. KEC

HOLMSLEY SOUTH, Hampshire

Station:	Station 455
Location:	West of Brockenhurst and the A35, east of Thorney Hill, Hampshire
Previously:	RAF from Sep 1942
Major Units:	See below
Afterwards:	Returned to the RAF Oct 1944, closed 1947

CONSOLIDATED B-24D Liberators of the 93rd Bomb Wing's 330th Bomb Squadron operated from Holmsley South October to December 1942 in the anti-submarine role. In June 1944 the B-26s of the 394th BG moved in from Boreham, Essex, to use Station 455 briefly as a forward base until going on to France – Tour-en-Bessin – in September.

A line-up of B-17s receiving attention at Honington. From the rear: unidentified; 96th Bomb Group, 338th Bomb Squadron, Snetterton Heath; 447th BG, Rattlesden; 100th BG, 349th BS, Thorpe Abbotts. US NATIONAL ARCHIVES

HONINGTON, Suffolk

Station:	375
Location:	South of Thetford, north of the village of Honington, between the A134 and A1088
Previously:	'Expansion period' station for the RAF, opened
Major Units:	Eighth Air Force, **364th Fighter Group** – P-38s and P-51s
	Code letters: 383rd Fighter Sqn 'NZ-', 384th FS '5Y-', 385th FS 'SE-'
Afterwards:	To the RAF Feb 1946 for extensive usage, mostly V-bombers all the way through to the last Tornados leaving in Feb 1994.
	Now Headquarters for the RAF Regiment.

HONINGTON'S FIRST role for the USAAF took advantage of the extensive hangars and facilities. Up to early 1944, the base was used for heavy maintenance of 3rd Air Division B-17 Flying Fortresses. As shown above, the flight line was always crowded with bombers awaiting attention.

Compared with facilities at other bases, the 364th Fighter Group could wallow in the opulence of an RAF 'Expansion Scheme' station for all of its time in the UK – February 1944 to November 1945. Honington was use as a frontline RAF base to 1994, it last being home to swing-wing Tornados. Many buildings from all eras of the statiion's illustrious past survive within the perimeter.

Our 'cover star', Lt Al Keeler with a 95th Bomb Group B-17G at Horham, 1944.
AL KEELER VIA WARREN E THOMPSON

HORHAM, Suffolk

Station:	119
Location:	East of Eye, north west of the village of Horham and north of the B1117
Previously:	Built for the USAAF, in use from Sep 1942
Major Units:	Eighth Air Force, **95th Bomb Group** – B-17s
	Group markings: B in a square
	Code letters: 334th Bomb Sqn 'BG-', 335th BS 'OE-', 336th BS 'ET-', 412th BS 'QW-'
Afterwards:	To the RAF Oct 1945. Sold off for agriculture 1962

HORHAM WAS home to A-20s of the 47th Bomb Group and B-26s of the 323rd BG from opening for short periods before accepting its main resident unit, the 95th BG, coming in from Framlingham in May 1943 The 95th was the first US unit to bomb Berlin and receive no less than three Distinguished Unit Citations before departing in July 1945.

The Red Feather Club is the official museum of the 95th Bomb Group, run by the 95th Bomb Group Heritage Association. It has brought back to life the former NCOs' club at USAAF Station 119 and included among the exhibits are the famous murals painted by S/Sgt Nathan Bindler. Open on the last Sunday of each month, May to October. More details: 01728 860930 **www.95thbg-horham.com**

HORSHAM ST FAITH, Norfolk

Station:	123
Location:	Present day Norwich Airport, access off the A140, north of Norwich
Previously:	Built for the RAF, 1939, extensive usage, mostly light bombers
Major Units:	Eighth Air Force, **56th Fighter Group** – P-47Cs from Apr 1943 until Jul 1943 which then moved to Halesworth
	Eighth Air Force: **458th Bomb Group** – B-24s Group markings: K in a circle Code letters: 752nd Bomb Sqn '7V-', 753rd BS 'J4-', 754th BS 'Z5-', 755th BS 'J3-'
Afterwards:	Returned to the RAF, extensive use, mostly fighters, up to Apr 1963. Became Norwich Airport Mar 1970. See also below

Three 458th Liberators, the two in the background from the 754th Bomb Squadron. In the foreground is B-24J 44-40066 of the 753rd Bomb Squadron. The B-24s to the left have 'toned-down' 'stars n' bars', which here appear almost black. US NATIONAL ARCHIVES

IN COMPARISON to many of the other airfields that personnel of the USAAF Eighth Air Force found themselves based at, Horsham St Faith offered substantial buildings, as befits a station built if not to 'Expansion' plans, but certainly towards them. The 56th Fighter Group was briefly a lodger while it awaited the permanent move to Halesworth. The B-24s ('Hs, 'Js, 'Ls and 'Ms were used) of the 458th were operational from March 1944 and their varied work included experimentation with Azon-guided bombs. The last mission was staged in late April 1945 and the USAAF was out of the airfield by July.

Less and less of the wartime buildings can be found as the airport grows and grows, but on the northern perimeter all of this is put to rights with the **City of Norwich Aviation Museum**. There is plenty on the 458th Bomb Group and the Eighth Air Force in and around the area and a wide array of aircraft and other exhibits. Open April to October, Tuesday to Sunday and Bank Holidays, November to March. More details: 01603 893080 **www.cnam.co.uk**

Five 458th Bomb Group B-24s near the Norfolk coast. 'J4-' codes on the left hand trio denote 753rd Bomb Squadron aircraft; 'Z5-' on the two on the right, the 754th BS. US NATIONAL ARCHIVES

Evacuating casualties from a 752nd Bomb Squadron at Horsham St Faith. US NATIONAL ARCHIVES

HURN, Dorset

Station:	492
Location:	North of Bournemouth and the B3073, west of the A338
Previously:	RAF from Jul 1941, used as a forward base
Major Units:	See below
Afterwards:	To RAF Oct 1944 and civil from 1945. From 1951 production and test flight centre for Vickers (Varsity), later BAC, BAC-111 production. Now major airliner maintenance and general aviation centre

WHAT IS today Bournemouth Airport had a varied World War Two and this included a variety of USAAF units using it for brief periods as a forward base. Most notable was the 397th Bomb Group and its B-26s moving in from Rivenhall, Essex, in August 1944 – transferring to France the following month. The P-61 Black Widows of the 422nd and 4235th Night Fighter Squadrons deployed to Hurn for anti-V-1 missions in July 1944.

On the southern perimeter of the airport, co-located with the Adventure Wonderland Theme Park is the Bournemouth Aviation Museum. Open daily, more details: 01202 473141
www.aviation-museum.co.uk

Night fighter 'ace' Lt Paul A Smith in cockpit of his 422nd Night Fighter Squadron P-61 'Lady Gen'. His victory tally shows five aerial 'kills', five locomotives and one V-1 destroyed. JOHN ANDERSON VIA WARREN E THOMPSON

Very rare colour air-to-air of a Northrop P-61 Black Widow. 'Warbash Cannon Ball IV' was assigned to the 425th Night Fighter Squadron's CO Major Leon 'Gilly' Lewis. This image was taken over France after D-Day while the squadron was operating out of Hurn. KARL SOUKIKIAN VIA WARREN E THOMPSON

IBSLEY, Hampshire

Station:	347
Location:	North of Ringwood, south east of Ibsley village and east of the A338
Previously:	RAF from Feb 1941
Major Units:	Eighth Air Force, **1st Fighter Group**, 71st FS and 94th FS – P-38s. To RAF Dec 1941. Ninth Air Force, **48th Fighter Group** – P-47s Code letters: 492nd Fighter Sqn 'F4-', 493rd FS 'I7-', 494th FS '6M-'
Afterwards:	To RAF Mar 1945, sold off 1947

THE P-38Fs of the 1st FG came in from Goxhill, Lincs, in August 1942 before redeploying to Algeria in November. The second 'occupation' was by Ninth Air Force P-47Ds in March 1944, for the work-up to D-Day, moving on to Deux Jumeaux in July 1944.

KEEVIL, Wiltshire

Station:	471
Location:	South of the A361, east of Trowbridge, Wiltshire
Previously:	USAAF from operational, Sep 1942
Major Units:	Twelfth Air Force, **62nd Troop Carrier Group** (4th, 7th, 8th, 51st TCSs) – C-47s and C-53s
Afterwards:	To RAF Jan 1944. USAF depot (non-flying) from 1955. Now used by RAF for exercises and also civilian gliding

WITH THEIR Douglas C-47s and C-53 Skytroopers, the 62nd TCG used Keevil as the launch-pad for its part in the invasion of North Africa, Operation TORCH, of November 1942. All went quiet beyond this until mid-1943 when a variety of USAAF units, including the 363rd Fighter Group used the airfield for brief sessions.

B-17F 230288 of Kimbolton's 525th Bomb Squadron, outside a hangar: note the tents. US NATIONAL ARCHIVES

KIMBOLTON, Cambridgeshire

Station: 117
Location: North of the village, south west of Stow Magna
Previously: RAF from Nov 1941, satellite of Molesworth. USAAF from Jun 1941
Major Units: Eighth Air Force, **379th Bomb Group** – B-17s
Group marking: K in a triangle
Code letters: 524th Bomb Sqn 'WA-', 525th BS 'FR-', 526th BS 'LF-', 527th BS 'FO-'
Afterwards: Returned to farmland by mid-1946. Little trace of the airfield today

THE B-17Gs of the 379th BG may well have welcomed the sight of Grafham Water (due east of the airfield), but that reservoir was not there during their tenure. The 379th's B-17s were not the first USAAF aircraft at Kimbolton however, the B-17Fs of the 91st BG were briefly housed there during the summer of 1942. To the 379th fell the honour of flying the largest number of operations – 330 – of any 'Mighty Eighth' bomb group. Arriving in June 1943, the unit left for North Africa in June 1945 and Kimbolton fell silent. Occasional light aircraft use was made of the airfield, but today little trace can be seen of its days as a bomber base.

Issued to Kimbolton's 379th Bomb Group in January 1945, B-17G 44-6915 served with the 524th BS. PETE WEST © 2013

A navigator at his position in a B-17. US NATIONAL ARCHIVES

King's Cliffe-based P-38J Lightning of the 20th Fighter Group's 55th Fighter Squadron. PETE WEST © 2013

A P-38 Lightning of the 20th Fighter Group at King's Cliffe in late 1943.
ART ROWLEY VIA WARREN E THOMPSON

Captain Max Pyles's Mustang of the 79th Fighter Squadron, 20th Fighter Group engine running at King's Cliffe. MAX PYLES VIA WARREN E THOMPSON

KING'S CLIFFE, Northamptonshire

Station:	367
Location:	North east of the village, south of the minor road to Wansford
Previously:	RAF from 1941, extensive use as fighter station
Major Units:	Eighth Air Force, **20th Fighter Group** – P-38s and P-51s
	Code letters: 55th Fighter Sqn 'KI-', 77th FS 'LC-', 79th FS 'MC-'
Afterwards:	Returned to RAF for non-flying duties, airfield to care and maintenance 1957 and sold off 1959

ON THE King's Cliffe to Wansford road, on what was the northern boundary of this famous fighter station, is a very impressive memorial that incorporates the wing of a Spitfire and a Mustang – encapsulating the activity at the airfield. In December 1942 for a brief period, the airfield had a foretaste of its USAAF life when the Bell P-39 and P-400 Airacobras of the 350th Fighter Group worked up before moving on to North Africa. In a similar manner, the P-47C Thunderbolts of the 56th Fighter Group were briefly in attendance from February 1943. It was the 20th Fighter Group that was to make King's Cliffe its own from August 1943. Initially equipped with long-ranging Lockheed P-38H and 'J Lightnings, the 20th made the transition to North American P-51D Mustangs from July 1944. The 20th departed in April 1945.

The dual-nationality King's Cliffe Memorial. KEY

RIGHT: **Lt R W Bebout, his crew chief and ground crew in front of 20th Fighter Group P-38 'Betsy VI' at King's Cliffe. The intake of the port engine carries the legend 'Pride of Pershing Square' a well-known New York eatery.** US NATIONAL ARCHIVES

A B-17G of the 388th Bomb Group receiving attention at Knettishall. USAFA VIA WARREN E THOMPSON

KINGSNORTH, Kent

Station:	418
Location:	South of Ashford, east of the A2070, south west of the village of South Stour
Previously:	RAF ALG from Jul 1943
Major Units:	Ninth Air Force, **36th Fighter Group** – P-47s Code letters: 22nd Fighter Sqn '3T-', 23rd FS '7U-', 53rd FS '6V-'
Afterwards:	Returned to farmland Sep 1944

RAF SPITFIRES first used the Kingsnorth Advanced Landing Ground, followed by the 36th's P-47s in April 1944, which moved on to Brucheville, France, leaving the remains of the temporary airfield to be ripped up and removed.

KINGSTON BAGPUIZE, Berkshire

Station:	403
Location:	West of Abingdon and south west of the village, Berks
Previously:	RAF from operational, Jan 1942
Major Units:	See below
Afterwards:	To RAF Dec 1944 as storage site until 1954

THE LOCALS pronounce this 'Bagpoise'. USAAF IXth Air Force Command took on the airfield for a series of operational trials up to August 1944. For some of the time, the airfield was coated in a wire mesh and fighter units were deployed to see how this improved 'ops'.

During the trials, no less than 50 P-47 Thunderbolts were deployed to Station 403 on March 10, 1944. These were from the 368th Fighter Group at Chilbolton, Hampshire. On the following day, the P-47s flew normal missions from the new surface, to give it a real operational evaluation. More trials in April proved that the mesh needed constant patching and that is was far 'higher maintenance' than had been hoped.

KIRTON-IN-LINDSEY, Lincolnshire

Station:	349
Location:	South of the village, north of the B1205
Previously:	RFC/RAF station 1916-1919. RAF station from May 1940 – mostly fighters
Major Units:	See below
Afterwards:	Remained occupied by the RAF, closed to service flying in 1965. Active gliding site

THE AIRFIELD had a very active career mainly with RAF fighters, but it also briefly held USAAF units while they worked up – hence it being given the 'Station 349' label. The P-38s of the 1st Fighter Group arrived in mid-1942 and from October to December of that year, the P-39 Airacobras of the 81st Fighter Group were also resident.

KNETTISHALL, Suffolk

Station:	136
Location:	South east of Thetford, south of the village of Knettishall and off the A1066
Previously:	Built for the RAF 1943 but transferred to the USAAF in Jun 1943 with no major RAF usage
Major Units:	Eighth Air Force, **388th Bomb Group** – B-17s Group markings: H in a square 560th, 561st, 562nd and 563rd BSs – no codes used
Afterwards:	To RAF Oct 1945, no flying usage. Sold off 1957. Many features remain to be seen and a small airstrip is maintained

AS WELL as uniquely shunning the adoption of squadron codes, the 388th is best known for its 'parenting' of Project APHRODITE, the use of B-17s and B-24s as flying bombs and for Project BATTY, the development of TV-guided weapons, but these were carried out on detachment at Fersfield, Norfolk. The 388th was resident June 1943 to August 1945.

LAKENHEATH, Suffolk

Location: South west of Brandon, west of the A1065
Previously: RAF from Mar 1941, mostly Bomber Command. To the USAF Aug 1948
Major Units: See text
Afterwards: Major USAF Europe base, home to the 48th Fighter Wing – 492nd, 493rd and 494th Fighter Sqns – 492nd and 494th with McDonnell Douglas F-15E Strike Eagles, 493rd with F-15C and 'D Eagles

Despite the extensive developments that have taken place since 1952, the three-runway origins of Lakenheath are still apparent. KEY–STEVE FLETCHER

THE USAF first used Lakenheath from August 1948, and up to 1959 it was used for the rotation of Strategic Air Command Bomb Groups on rotation to the UK. In its time, 'The Heath' thundered to Boeing B-29 and B-50 Superfortresses; Convair B-36 Pacemakers, North American B-45 Tornados and Boeing B-47 Stratojets as well as the many transports and Boeing KC-97 Stratofreighter tankers needed to support such deployments. The base received massive engineering work in 1952 that reshaped it so that its RAF origins became increasingly less apparent. In January 1960 the 48th Tactical Fighter Wing (492nd, 493rd and 494th TFSs) arrived from France, because that country was no longer happy with the US and NATO and its North American F-100D Super Sabres became very familiar sights. Little did the 48th realise that it would remain in the UK for half a century plus! In 1971 the 'Huns' were replaced by F-4Ds and in March 1977 the first General Dynamics F-111F swing-bombers arrived. The F-111s took part in the bombing of Libya in April 1986. The F-15Cs and 'Ds arrived in February 1992 and the unit moved from being a TFW to an FW at much the same time, with F-15E Strike Eagles later taking the dominant role. The 48th FW took part in DESERT STORM and the second Iraqi conflict. Within the base is a visitor centre and memorial park – the Wings of Liberty Memorial Park – but please note that access to this is by prior permission only.

F-111Fs of the 48th Tactical Fighter Wing on finals for Lakenheath. KEY-DUNCAN CUBITT

LANGAR, Nottinghamshire

Station: 490
Location: In the Vale of Belvoir, north west of Harby
Previously: RAF from Sep 1942
Major Units: Ninth Air Force, **435th Troop Carrier Group** – C-47s and C-53s
Code letters: 75th Troop Carrier Sqn 'SH-', 76th TCS 'CW-', 77th TCS 'IB-', 78th TCS 'CM-'
Ninth Air Force, **441st Troop Carrier Group** – C-47s, C-53s
Code letters: 99th Troop Carrier Sqn '3J-', 100th TCS '8C-', 301st TCS 'Z4-', 302nd TCS '2L-'
Afterwards: Returned to RAF Sep 1944. RCAF based 1952 to 1963. Parachute school and light aviation to present

WEEKENDS AND some weekdays, the area glories in the sound of aircraft climbing to height for yet another drop of sport parachutists. This use of the airfield reflects its days with the USAAF when paratroopers were the order of the day in C-47 Skytrains and C-53 Skytroopers. Two Troop Carrier Groups flew from the airfield; the 435th from October 1943 to January 1944 and the 441st, January to April 1944. Langar was also used for the erection and flight test of Waco CG-4 assault gliders up to May 1944.

The unusual tower at Langford Lodge, Northern Ireland. KEY-KEN ELLIS

LANGFORD LODGE, Northern Ireland

Station: 597
Location: West of Crumlin, on Gartree Point
Previously: No use prior to USAAF from Jun 1942
Major Units: 3rd Base Air Depot
Afterwards: Returned to RAF Mar 1946

A HUGE construction programme, including a single track railway spur, created this vast base. Along with Burtonwood (1st BAD) and Warton (2nd BAD), Langford Lodge was essentially a huge factory supporting every facet of the USAAF's operations, from instrument overhaul to airframe modification. The 3rd BAD operated a satellite at Greencastle. By late 1944 work here moved from 'production' to storage and by May 1945 nearly 600 aircraft were parked out. Today the airfield is much as it was when the BAD stopped operating in August 1945. Ejection seat trials and development engineering are undertaken and a runway is kept in good health and occasionally used.

At Play

BELOW: **Glenn Miller and his band performing outside a hangar during the summer of 1944.**

Underlining the 'Overpaid, Oversexed and Over Here' image, strenuous efforts were made to make life across the ocean tolerable, as these images from Wattisham testify

Entertainment came in all forms: on stage at the 'Red Cross Club'.

The Motor Pool had a plentiful stock of Jeeps, and jaunts off into town were relatively easy to arrange.

Bob Hope regaling an attentive audience

LEFT: **Although Wattisham was built as an 'Expansion Period' RAF station, as the population of the base expanded, many buildings were much more rudimentary: the 'Little Wheels Club', 1944.**

RIGHT: **With pin-ups adorning the walls, life in the airmen's barracks, included desks, and coffee readily at hand.**

ABOVE: **A dance, probably in the NCO Club.**

FAR LEFT: **The Enlisted Men's Mess Hall, ready for Christmas Day, 1944.**

LEFT: **'Chow time' in the Enlisted Men's Mess Hall.** ALL KEC

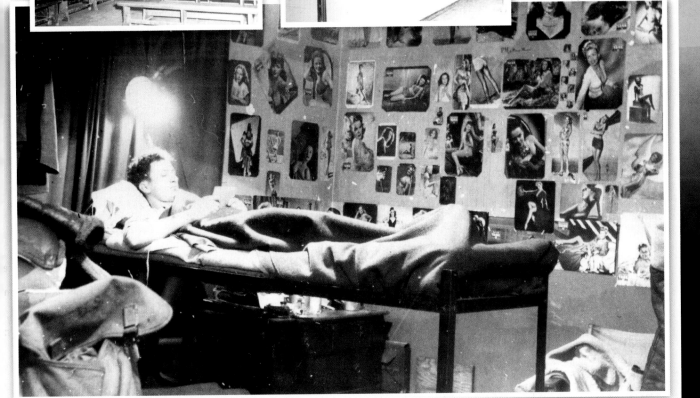

Unarmed, Unafraid and in Harm's Way

A pilot tinkering with the engine of his L-4 at a USAAF bomber base. KEC

A familiar sight from 1943 through to the end of the war in Europe were the Piper L-4 Grasshoppers, Stinson L-5 Sentinels and other 'L-Birds' operated for the US Army as air observation posts and for communications duties. Capable of landing in very confined spaces, 'L-Birds' were based at many strips close to concentrations of US Army troops and at regional headquarters - far too numerous and diverse to list within this special publication.

From D-Day, L-4s were among the first assets brought into Normandy. Along with British Austers, these unarmed, low- and slow-flying 'eyes in the sky' became most feared by the Wehrmacht as they could direct artillery to any targets they spotted.

LASHENDEN, Kent

Station:	410
Location:	Between Smarden Bell and the A274, south of Headcorn
Previously:	RAF Advanced Landing Ground from Aug 1943
Major Units:	Ninth Air Force, **354th Fighter Group** – P-51s Code letters: 353rd Fighter Sqn 'FT-', 355th FS 'GQ-', 356th FS 'AJ-'
Afterwards:	Returned to farmland Jan 1945. Light aviation from 1973

THE 354th, operating P-51B Mustangs initially, carried out a variety of work, including bomber escort and anti-V-1 missions, as well as tactical attacks. The unit moved on to Criqueville, France, in June 1944. In 1973 the land came to life again as an aerodrome and it still thrives, being home to – among others –the Tiger Club. Please note, although it has been called Headcorn since the 1970s, it has no connection to the wartime Headcorn airfield – see earlier.

The **Lashenden Air Warfare Museum**, which is busy expanding its buildings, contains a rich treasure trove of material on the USAAF at the base and in the county, and much, much more. Open weekends and Bank Holidays in June, July and August, plus Sundays March to May and September to December. More details: 01622 631799 **www.lashendenairwarfaremuseum.co.uk**

Present-day Headcorn aerodrome is based upon Station 410 Lashenden. The Air Warfare Museum is located bottom left KEY

'Chief Wapello', B-24H 42-252618 of the 487th Bomb Group's 839th Bomb Squadron taxying past the signals square at Lavenham. VIA BILL MORTON

LAVENHAM, Suffolk

Station:	137
Location:	North west of the delightful village of Lavenham, between the A1141 and the A134
Previously:	Built for the USAAF, 1943
Major Units:	Eighth Air Force, **487th Bomb Group** – B-24s and B-17s Group markings: P in a square Code letters: 836th Bomb Sqn '2G-', 837th BS '4F-', 838th BS '2C-', 839th BS 'R5-'
Afterwards:	To the RAF Oct 1945, various, non-flying uses to 1948. Sold off and returned to agriculture 1958. Much remains, including the control tower

THE 487th had a brief but busy time while at Lavenham, taking the rare step of converting from Liberators to Flying Fortresses in the already hectic summer of 1944. After the RAF left, the airfield was used occasionally for light aviation, and as readers of the October and November issues will know, it was briefly home to Lancaster VII NX611 (G-ASXX) – today's *Just Jane*.

LEISTON, Suffolk

Station	373
Location:	North west of the village of Leiston – also known as Saxmundham and Theberton
Previously:	Built for the USAAF, 1943
Major Units:	Eighth Air Force, **357th Fighter Group** – P-51s Code letters: 362nd Fighter Sqn 'G4-', 363rd FS 'B6-', 364th FS 'C5-'
Afterwards:	To the RAF Oct 1945, closed and returned to agriculture 1946

FIRST UNIT to inhabit Leiston was the 358th Fighter Group flying P-47Ds from December 1943 to January 1944 when it took on, in turn, P-51Bs, 'Cs, 'Ds and 'Ks up to July 1945. The 357th was the first P-51B unit in the Eighth Air Force and went on to earn two Distinguished Unit Citations. Little remains of the airfield but from 1983, it has been used for flight testing of the locally-manufactured CFM Shadow light aircraft.

The tower survives at Little Staughton. KEN ELLIS

LITTLE STAUGHTON, Bedfordshire

Station:	127
Location:	West of St Neots, south east of the village
Previously:	Scant RAF usage late 1942, USAAF from Nov 1942
Major Units:	B-17 and other types for maintenance and ferrying
Afterwards:	To the RAF Mar 1944 and earned great fame as a Pathfinder Force base.

TO CARE and maintenance Dec 1945. Post-war used for overhaul contract work for RAF, now light aviation.

Time Will Not Diminish The Glory of Their Deeds

Set in 30 acres, the Cambridge American Cemetery and Memorial at Madingley is an impressive and reflective place of pilgrimage. KEY-STEVE FLETCHER

★ The words of General John J Pershing sum up the purpose of the Cambridge American Cemetery and Memorial at Madingley, west of Cambridge, which opened in 1956. Within its 30 acres 3,812 US combat personnel are buried and another 5,127 are recorded on the Tablets of the Missing. Administered by the American Battle Monuments Commission, in August 2012 construction of a new $4m visitor centre commenced, and is due to have opened by the time these words are read. Located off the A1303 west of Cambridge, it is open daily, for more details take a look at **www.abmc.gov**

P-51D 'Cooter' of the 357th Fighter Group fuelling up at Leiston. JIM FRARY VIA WARREN E THOMPSON

P-51Ds of the 375th Fighter Squadron, led by Colonel Tom Christian's 'Lou IV'.
US NATIONAL ARCHIVES

LITTLE WALDEN, Essex

Station:	165
Location:	North of Saffron Walden on the B1052 – also known as Hadstock
Previously:	USAAF from operational, Mar 1944
Major Units:	Ninth Air Force, **409th Bomb Group** – A-20s Code letters: 640th Bomb Sqn 'W5-', 641st BS '7G-', 642nd BS 'D6-', 643rd BS '5I-' Eighth Air Force, **361st Fighter Group** – P-51s Code letters: 374th Fighter Sqn 'B7-', 375th FS 'E2-', 376th FS 'E9-'
Afterwards:	Airfield closed Jan 1946

UNLIKE MANY Essex airfields, Little Walden had a varied occupancy. The A-20s of the 409th moved to Bretigny, France, in September 1944. The P-51Ds of the 361st were based twice. The unit moved to St Dizier, France, in October 1944 and then to Chievres, Belgium, returning in April 1945. In the intervening period, B-17s from Debach, Suffolk, 'bolt-holed' while their base was under maintenance. The 361st finally left in November 1945. The Little Walden to Hadstock road was closed during the war, those travelling on it today drive through the middle of the former airfield and much can be seen, including the tower.

LYMINGTON, Hampshire

Station:	551
Location:	East of Lymington, south east of Walhampton and the B3054
Previously:	USAAF ALG from Mar 1944
Major Units:	Ninth Air Force, **50th Fighter Group** – P-47s Code letters: 10th Fighter Sqn 'T5-', 81st FS '2N-', 313th FS 'W3-'
Afterwards:	Reverted to farmland Sep 1944

LOOKING OUT over the Solent and the Lymington River, a basic and very short-lived Advanced Landing Ground. After a three-month stay, the 50th moved on to Carentan in France in June 1944

MANSTON, Kent

Location:	West of Ramsgate, on the A253
Previously:	RNAS from 1951, RAF from 1918
Major Units:	See below
Afterwards:	To RAF and civil control Apr 1959. Now Kent International Airport, plus extensive aviation maintenance, general aviation and small RAF enclave

THE USAF moved into Manston from July 1950 for very nearly a decade of intensive operations. The first unit, the 20th Fighter Bomber Wing (FBW), flew F-84E Thunderjets on detachment, with other units following suit. From November 1951 the base was a USAF Europe facility and the resident unit became the 406th FBW, also flying F-84Es. The 406th later re-equipped with the F-86D Sabre and became a Fighter Interceptor Wing at the same time (with constituent units the 512th, 513th and 514th Fighter Squadrons). From 1950, rescue cover was supplied by the 9th Air Rescue Squadron (ARS) with Grumman SA-16 Albatrosses and even a few Boeing SB-29 Superfortresses. In 1952 the unit was renumbered the 66th ARS. From April 1956 Manston became a Master Diversion Airfield, a military role it held well into the 1970s. From April 1959 the US units pulled out and the airfield became a mixed RAF/civil operation.

ABOVE: **The RAF Manston History Museum includes much material on the airfield's American past.** KEN ELLIS

BELOW LEFT: **Grumman SA-16 Albatrosses were based at Manston with the 9th and then the 67th Air Rescue Squadron.** KEC

BELOW RIGHT: **The purpose-built Spitfire and Hurricane Museum includes the popular 'Merlin Cafeteria'.** KEN ELLIS

Manston has two superb museums, the first to be established being the **Spitfire and Hurricane Memorial Museum**. There is a wealth of material to see and the superb 'Merlin Cafeteria' to sample. Open daily, check for seasonal variations: 01843 821940 **www.spitfiremuseum.org.uk**

The **RAF Manston History Museum** is located in the old MT building and is run by the RAF Manston History Society. It concentrates on the 90-year history of Manston, both military and civil. Open daily, check for seasonal variations: 01843 825224 **www.rafmanston.co.uk**

View from the tower at Martlesham Heath, 1944 and 2013. Mustangs of the 356th Fighter Group parked out, with examples from the 360th Fighter Squadron closest to the tower. INSET: Today, it's cars that use the hard-standings. US NATIONAL ARCHIVES VIA WARREN E THOMPSON / KEN ELLIS

MARTLESHAM HEATH, Suffolk

Station:	369
Location:	South east of Martlesham, the A12 cuts through the site
Previously:	Built for the RFC 1916, then to the RAF with long-time association with the Aeroplane & Armament Experimental Establishment. To the USAAF Sep 1943
Major Units:	Eighth Air Force, **356th Fighter Group** – P-47s and P-51s Code letters: 359th Fighter Sqn 'OC-', 360th FS 'PI-', 361st FS 'QI-' USAF non-flying presence 1955-1986
Afterwards:	To the RAF Dec 1945 for a variety of uses, including trials and experimentation. Last flying units left in 1963. Many buildings can be seen within the industrial and retail areas

AN INDUSTRIAL/RETAIL complex and multi-lane bypass that straddles most of the former airfield, but the tower museum flies the flag for the incredible heritage of this airfield. In the summer of 1943 runways went down for the first time and the USAAF moved in with the 356th Fighter Group – which suffered greater losses to claimed victories than any other Eighth Air Force unit. The 356th first used P-47Ds from October 1943, converting to P-51Ds and 'Ks in November 1944; it left in November 1945.

Martlesham's tower is lovingly preserved and home to a first-rate museum. KEN ELLIS

The vista of a control tower, complete with its signals square, amid a housing estate is quite surreal. Run by the **Martlesham Heath Aviation Society**, the **Control Tower Museum**, contains a vast amount of material on an exceptional airfield with an incredible heritage. The car park for the museum was once a series of revetments where the P-47s and P-51s of the USAAF's 356th Fighter Group used to park. Open every Sunday, April to October. More details: 01473 624510 or 01473 435104 **www.mhas.org.uk**

On the southern edge of the former airfield in a cavernous building, which was known to the USAF as 'The Roc' and last used by the 2164th Communications Squadron in the early 1990s, it is now the home of the **Suffolk Aviation Heritage Centre**. Open Sundays and Bank Holidays, more details: 01473 711275 **www.suffolkaviationheritage.org.uk**

P-47D 226272 'Angel Eyes' of the 361st Fighter Squadron, 356th Fighter Group based at Martlesham Heath escorting a B-24. US NATIONAL ARCHIVES

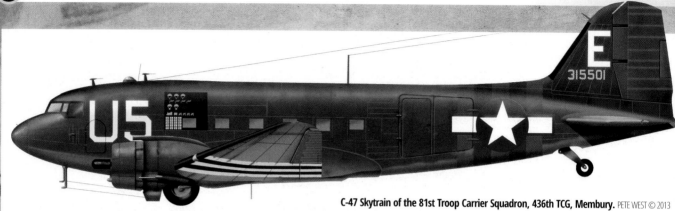

C-47 Skytrain of the 81st Troop Carrier Squadron, 436th TCG, Membury. PETE WEST © 2013

MATCHING, Essex

Station:	166
Location:	North of Chipping Ongar, east of Matching Green
Previously:	USAAF from operational, Feb 1944
Major Units:	Ninth Air Force, **391st Bomb Group** – B-26s
	Code letters: 572nd Bomb Sqn 'P2-', 573rd BS 'T6-', 574th BS '4L-', 575th BS 'O8-'
	391st to Roye-Amy, France, Sep 1944.
Afterwards:	To RAF Oct 1944, flying ceased Oct 1945. Substantial elements of the airfield still to be seen

The M4 and its service station cuts through the northern perimeter of what was Station 466. KEY

MENDLESHAM, Suffolk

Station:	156
Location:	East of the village of Mendlesham and east of the A140
Previously:	Built for the RAF 1943, used by fighter units. To the USAAF Mar 1944
Major Units:	Eighth Air Force, **34th Bomb Group** – B-24s and B-17s
	Group marking: S in square
	Code letters: 4th Bomb Sqn '3L-', 7th BS 'R2-', 18th BS '8I-', 391st BS 'Q6-'
Afterwards:	To the RAF late 1945, used as an MU 1950-1952. Sold off in 1954. Runway and perimeter patterns remain, plus some buildings

THE 34th Bomb Group started life in January 1941 with B-17s and as such was to become the oldest bomb group to form a part of the Eighth Air Force. It arrived in the UK and flew B-24Hs and 'J from April 1944, moving to B-17Gs in August 1944. Today the airfield is largely used by light industry and is dominated by a large radio mast.

'Fifinella' and crew of the 391st Bomb Group, 575th Bomb Squadron, Matching, August 1944. US NATIONAL ARCHIVES

MEMBURY, Berkshire

Station:	466
Location:	South of Lambourn, close to the Membury services on the M4
Previously:	USAAF from operational, Aug 1942
Major Units:	Eighth Air Force, 67th Observation Group, later **67th Recce Group** – Spitfire Vs
	52nd Fighter Group (12th, 107th, 109th and 153rd Sqns) – Spitfire Vs;
	Ninth AF, **436th Troop Carrier Group** – C-47s
	Code letters: 79th Troop Carrier Sqn 'S6-', 80th TCS '7D-', 81st TCS 'U5-', 82nd TCS '3D-'
Afterwards:	To the RAF Jul 1945 and closed Apr 1947

THE SPITFIRE units trained up early USAAF recce units. The 436th arrived in March 1944 and moved elements of the 101st Airborne to D-Day and was involved in each of the major airborne assaults thereafter. It moved to France in February 1945.

From the air, Metfield takes some studying, before traces of the three-runway layout start to manifest themselves. KEY

MERRYFIELD, Somerset

Station:	464 – also known as Isle Abbotts
Location:	North west of Ilminster, east of the A358, Somerset
Previously:	USAAF from operational, Feb 1944
Major Units:	Ninth Air Force, **441st Troop Carrier Group** – C-47s and CG-4As
	Code letters: 99th Troop Carrier Sqn '3J-' , 100th TCS '8C-', 301st TCS 'Z4-', 302nd TCS '2L-'
Afterwards:	To RAF Nov 1944 – see below

BEFORE THE airfield opened, it changed its name from that of a village immediately to the north to one that defies local geography. The 441st took elements of the US 82nd and 101st Airborne Divisions to D-Day. With the establishment of the beachhead, re-supply flights by the 441st also brought wounded back to the extensive field hospital established at Merryfield. The airfield closed as a RAF station in 1946, only to re-open in November 1951 for training. Westland also used the airfield for helicopter flight test. It later became a satellite for nearby RNAS Yeovilton and is still used by Merlin and Sea King helicopters.

METFIELD, Suffolk

Station:	366
Location:	South east of the village of Metfield, north of the B1123
Previously:	Built for the USAAF 1943
Major Units:	Eighth Air Force, **353rd Fighter Group** – P-47s
	Code letters: 350th Fighter Sqn 'LH-', 351st FS 'YJ-', 352nd FS 'SX-'
	Eighth Air Force, **491st Bomb Group** 'The Ringmasters' – B-24s
	Group markings: Z in a circle
	Code letters: 852nd Bomb Sqn '3Q-', 853rd BS 'T8-', 854th BS '6X-', 855th BS 'V2-'
Afterwards:	To RAF 1945, sold off by 1950

RIGHT: **P-47D of the 352nd Fighter Squadron, 353rd FG, based at Metfield and later Raydon.**
© PETE WEST 2013 2013

TOP: **Assembly ships were brightly coloured 'Pied Pipers' helping to get each group's bomber stream into order and off on course. B-24D 42-40722 'The Little Gramper' of Metfield's 491st BG certainly caught the eye.** PETE WEST © 2013

ABOVE: **The last assembly ship to serve the 491st Bomb Group was B-24J 44-40101 'Tubarao'.** PETE WEST © 2013

Metfield's memorial has a base that shows the runway layout. KEY

AS THE Thunderbolts of the 353rd left for Raydon, Suffolk, in April 1944, Metfield prepared to take on a Bomb Group, in this case the 491st – 'The Ringmasters' – with B-24Hs, 'Js, 'Ls and 'Ms from August 1944 to July 1945. From August of that year other types could be seen on the airfield, all the way through to the end of flying in the summer of 1945 – Douglas C-54 Skymaster and C-47 Skytrain transports shuttling to and from the US East Coast and around the UK, respectively.

An F-6C Mustang of 15th TRS at Middle Wallop in 1944 with Lt Colonel Robert Simpson standing by the cockpit.
JACK WOOLNER VIA WARREN E THOMPSON

MIDDLE WALLOP, Hampshire

Station:	449
Location:	South west of Andover on the A343, north of Middle Wallop, Hampshire
Previously:	RAF from Apr 1940
Major Units:	Ninth Air Force, **67th Tactical Reconnaissance Group** – see below for details, Mar to Aug 1944
Afterwards:	Returned to RAF Aug 1944, to Army Air Corps 1957 and today HQ of AAC with a wide range of types

MIDDLE WALLOP'S foray into the realms of the USAAF came from August 1943 when it was allocated to the Americans. The 67th TRG was a complex unit with the following elements at 'Wallop: 12th TRS (coded 'ZM-') with Supermarine Spitfires and F-6 Mustangs; 15th TRS (Spitfires and F-6s) disbanding June 1944; 30th PRS ('I6-') with Lockheed F-5 and P-38 Lightnings; 107th TRS ('AX-', Spitfires and F-6s) and the 109th TRS ('VX-', Spitfires and F-6s). By August 1944 all but the 15th had moved on, to La Molay in France.

Middle Wallop is home to the **Museum of Army Flying**. Open daily: 01264 784421 **www.armyflying.com**

MILDENHALL, Suffolk

Location:	North west of the 'village' of Mildenhall, south of the A1101 – also known as Beck Row
Previously:	Built for the RAF 1933 – mostly Bomber Command operations throughout World War Two. USAF from July 1950
Major Units:	See text
Afterwards:	Huge USAF Europe base, acting as transport hub for flights from the USA; tanker and special operations units based

WHEN MILDENHALL was allocated to the USAF in 1950 it was used for bomber deployments to the UK and from 1951 these were flown under the aegis of Strategic Air Command. The first rotation was the 93rd Bomb Group's B-50Ds in 1950 with B-29s and B-47s and tanker-transport KC-97s thereafter. From 1959 the base took on an increasing transport role as Burtonwood, Lancs, was wound down as the transatlantic terminal for Military Air Transport Service and other traffic. In rough order of appearance, the base has witnessed intensive flying from C-47s, C-121 Constellations, C-118 Liftmasters, C-124 Globemaster IIs, C-133 Cargomasters, C-141 Starlifters, C-5 Galaxies and C-17 Globemaster IIIs. From 1966 Lockheed C-130E and 'H deployments were also made on a large scale through 'The

Hall' although by the early 1990s these had greatly diminished. From 1964, the US Navy established a transport facility using C-45 Expediters and C-117Ds which later gave way to Beech C-12s. From 1965 Boeing EC-135 airborne command posts began to be based and from January 1970 these were formalised under the 10th Airborne Command and Communications Squadron, which operated up to 1992. Other 'electronic' versions of the Stratotanker have also operated from Mildenhall, RC-135s being frequent visitors. From 1970 the base became a permanent home to a wing of KC-135 tankers, and 15 KC-135Rs are based today with the 100th Air Refueling Wing; KC-10 Extenders are also to be seen. From the early 1970s through to 1990 Mildenhall was also home to a detachment of the 9th Strategic Reconnaissance Wing, with up to two Lockheed SR-71A Blackbirds and attendant KC-135Qs undertaking long-range flights deep into Europe, the Middle East and beyond. In September 1994, with the wind down of Alconbury, Cambs, the 352nd Special Operations Group also moved into 'The Hall' and is still resident. Within the 352nd are the 7th Special Operations Squadron (SOS) with C-130Hs and MC-130Hs; the 21st SOS with Sikorsky MH-53M 'Super Jolly' rescue helicopters and the 67th SOS with MC-130P tankers.

The KC-135R Stratotankers of the 100th Air Refueling Wing proudly carry the D in a Square of the 100th Bomb Group, based at Thorpe Abbotts seven decades ago. KEY

Mildenhall is a vast and complex base, but traces of the wartime three-runway pattern can still be discerned. KEY

C in a triangle marking on the starboard wing; a 'Hell's Angels' B-17G at dispersal, March 1944. US NATIONAL ARCHIVES

Lt Benham and his crew in front of B-17 'The Floose' of the 303rd's 358th Bomb Squadron, Molesworth, May 1944. US NATIONAL ARCHIVES

MOLESWORTH, Cambridgeshire

Station:	107
Location:	North of the A14, east of Thrapston
Previously:	RAF from May 1941, varied usage. USAAF from June 1942
Major Units:	Eighth Air Force, **303rd Bomb Group** 'Hell's Angels' – B-17s Group markings: C in a triangle Code letters: 358th Bomb Sqn 'VS-', 359th BS 'BN-', 360th BS 'PU-', 427th BS 'GN-'
Afterwards:	To RAF from Jul 1945 and care and maintenance in late 1946. For USAF use, see below

USING DOUGLAS A-20 Havocs supplemented by RAF Bostons, the 15th BG staged the USAAF's first European bombing raid from Molesworth on June 29, 1942. The 15th, and a couple of other units were fleeting tenants here. Initially with B-17Fs, the 303rd BG – the famed 'Hell's Angels' – arrived in November 1942. Later taking on B-17Gs, the unit was the first to reach 300 operations. It left for North Africa in April 1945.

Molesworth's second US phase, one that still continues, started in July 1951 when the USAF moved in. First resident was the 582nd Air Re-Supply Group, operating an eclectic mix of aircraft, including Boeing B-29A Superfortresses, Grumman SA-16 Albatrosses and others. The unit's title was, shall we say, not the most accurate and many regard the unit as post-war 'Carpetbaggers', undertaking 'cloak-and-dagger' missions as well as air-sea rescue and other work. From October 1956, the 582nd became the 42nd Troop Carrier Squadron with Fairchild C-119 Flying Boxcars among other types. It moved to Alconbury in 1957. Other use – storage, maintenance, administrative occupied Molesworth until in the 1980s it became the central distribution site for the USAF's Tomahawk ground-launched cruise-missile system. They'd gone by the early 1990s and today Molesworth is home to the United States European Command's Joint Analysis Center, and 'parents' the enclave at nearby Alconbury.

Famous image from Molesworth's illustrious wartime history – Brig Gen Robert B Williams, 1st Air Division Commander, bidding farewell, care of a specially-signed 303rd BG Fortress, 1945. KEC

Wolfpack

Warren E Thompson profiles
the mighty Thunderbolts of
the 56th Fighter Group

Known as the 'Wolfpack', the 56th
Fighter Group destroyed more aircraft in air
combat than any other Eighth Air Force unit – 674 'kills'. It had
more 'aces' than any other USAAF group, including the top-scorer,
Colonel Francis S Gabreski. 'Gabby' had 28 confirmed victories and went
on to bag another 6.5 in Korea. BILL HESS VIA WARREN E THOMPSON

P-47 'Belle of Belmont' taxies past the base's photographer at Boxted, 1944. USAAF VIA WARREN E THOMPSON

Close-up of P-47D 42-26298 of the 56th's 62nd Fighter Squadron at Boxted, 1944. On the cowling it carried an image of cartoon star Donald Duck behind bars with the legend: 'Stalag Luft III – I Wanted Wings'. This was the infamous Sagan prisoner of war camp, venue of the 'Great Escape'. The P-47's name was 'Button Nose' carried on the fuselage side. USAAF VIA WARREN E THOMPSON

The 56th Fighter Group was the only Eighth Air Force outfit to fly Republic's big Thunderbolt throughout the war. Illustrated is P-47 'Shack Rat' at rest at Boxted. USAAF VIA WARREN E THOMPSON

Yellow rudders and the code letters 'LM-' define these Boxted-based Thunderbolts as belonging to the 56th's 62nd Fighter Squadron. USAAF VIA WARREN E THOMPSON

Revolutionary Spirit

Crew members of the 388th Bomb Group's 562nd Bomb Squadron preparing to board their B-17F, 42-30793 'Tom Paine', at Knettishall in Suffolk. Underneath the name is a famous line, written by Paine: "Tyranny, like Hell, is not easily conquered!" The kick at fascism is obvious, but it was actually written to inspire the Americans to declare independence from Great Britain in 1776! US NATIONAL ARCHIVES

NEW MILITARY AVIATION WEBSITE

AirForces *DAILY*

From the **AirForces Monthly News Team**, it's the **NEW** online military aviation news channel and reference resource. Available by subscription only, members receive access to exclusive online content, including:

- **Breaking News Reports**
- **Searchable Attrition Database Going Back to 2000**
- **Exclusive Articles and Features**
- **Combat Ops, Exercises and Training**
- **Insider Reports, Video and Photos**
- **Air Force Reports and Independent Surveys**

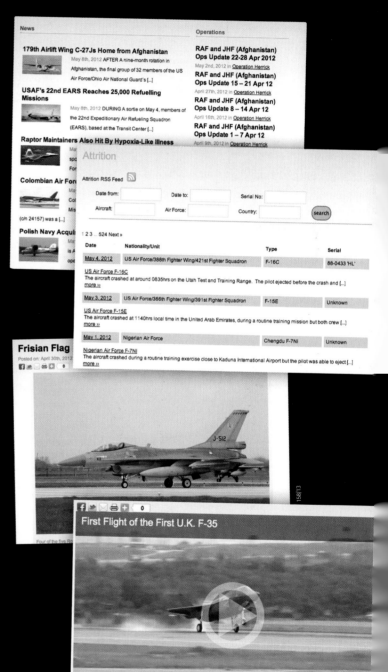

Access to all this exclusive content starts from £4.99 per month, with further discounts for Key Publishing magazine subscribers and longer term subscriptions.

Prices	Standard	Subscribers
Monthly	£4.99	£2.49
Six Monthly	£19.99	£9.99
Yearly	£34.99	£14.99

KEY

FREE 4 HOUR TRIAL*

To take advantage of this offer, register now at:
www.airforcesdaily.com

IT'S MILITARY AVIATION AT YOUR FINGERTIPS!

*Terms and Conditions apply, see website for full details. Offer valid until 31 December 2013

MOUNT FARM, Oxfordshire

Station:	234
Location:	North of Dorchester, west of Drayton St Leonard
Previously:	RAF from July 1940. USAAF from Dec 1942
Major Units:	Eighth Air Force, **13th Photo Reconnaissance Group,** 13th, 14th, 22nd and 27th Photo Sqns, to Dec 1945 – P-38s, F-5s and Spitfires
Afterwards:	To RAF Dec 1945 and sold off in 1957

BY THE time the RAF moved out of Mount Farm, it was already a specialist photo-recce station and the USAAF continued the tradition. Types operated centred on the P-38/F-5 but also included Supermarine Spitfires and – for D-Day requirements – L-5 Sentinels.

A handful of 'temporary' wartime buildings are still to be found on Northolt's western boundary. KEY-KEN ELLIS

NORTHOLT, Greater London

Location:	West London, on the A40
Previously:	Military airfield from 1915
Major Units:	See below
Afterwards:	RAF station throughout World War Two and still major communications and transport airfield

NORTHOLT WAS used by USAAF communications and transport units late 1943 to December 1944. Post-war it was used by a variety of small communications units, both USAF and US Navy.

The tower still stands at North Witham. KEN ELLIS

The runways at North Witham amid the surreal backdrop of woodland. KEN ELLIS

NORTH PICKENHAM, Norfolk

Station:	143
Location:	South east of Swaffham, airfield was located between the B1077 and the village of North Pickenham
Previously:	Built for the USAAF, Dec 1943
Major Units:	Eighth Air Force, **492nd Bomb Group** – B-24s Group marking: U in a circle Code letters: 856th Bomb Sqn '5Z-', 857th BS '9H-', 858th BS '9A-', 859th BS 'X4-' Eighth Air Force, **491st Bomb Group** 'The Ringmasters' – B-24s Group marking: Z in a circle Code letters: 852nd Bomb Sqn '3Q-', 853rd BS 'T8-', 854th BS '6X-', 855th BS 'V2-'
Afterwards:	To the RAF, mostly for maintenance unit usage (including the USAF in the mid-1950s); RAF Thor IRBM site 1959-1963. Then to agriculture and light industry

THE 492nd 'numberplate' was used twice in the UK, the North Pickenham version suffered very heavy losses in 64 missions May to August 1944, with 51 B-24Hs and 'Js lost in that time. By August 1944, the USAAF needed another B-24 unit at Harrington, Northants, for 'Carpetbagger' clandestine operations and so the 492nd was effectively disbanded following its mauling, to be recreated in the new role. The 491st – 'The Ringmasters' – took over the airfield and flew B-24Hs, 'Js, 'Ls and 'Ms up to July 1945. The runways are still visible and the heavy concrete of the Thor site remains invulnerable.

NORTH WITHAM, Lincolnshire

Station:	479
Location:	South east of Colsterworth, south of the A151 and east of the A1
Previously:	Handed over to USAAF on completion, Feb 1944
Major Units:	Ninth Air Force, 9th Troop Carrier Command Pathfinder School, Mar 1944, renamed Pathfinder Group Provisional Sep 1944
Afterwards:	To RAF Jun 1945 for bomb storage

AS WELL as the Pathfinder School, the base was home to a wide range of non-flying 9th Air Force units as well as the Pathfinder unit which helped to spearhead each of the Troop Carrier Groups as they took part in D-Day and the other airborne operations. Because of the nature of the units at South Witham, they did not move out until April 1945.

Today, the airfield is enveloped within publically accessible woodland called Twyford Wood, giving the eerie vista of runways lined with forest. Concrete ramps and bays on the runways at first appear confusing, but these are from the days when the runways were used for the storage of tens of thousands of bombs awaiting decommissioning.

The grass between the runways provided a war-winning resource: a B-17G of the 603rd Bomb Squadron, 398th BG, taxies past technology of another era at Nuthampstead. US NATIONAL ARCHIVES

BELOW: The 453rd Bomb Group's 'XO', actor James Stewart, awaiting the return of the B-24s. He clocked up 22 missions during his time with the 453rd. KEC

BOTTOM: Mimicking the tails of the resident 453rd Bomb Group's Liberators, Old Buckenham's impressive memorial. KEY

NUTHAMPSTEAD, Hertfordshire

Station:	131
Location:	East of the B1368, south east of Barkway
Previously:	Brief RAF use, USAAF from Sep 1943
Major Units:	Eighth Air Force, **55th Fighter Group** – P-38s then P-51s
	Code letters: 38th Fighter Sqn 'CG-', 338th FS 'CL-', 343rd FS 'CY-'
	Eighth Air Force, **398th Bomb Group** – B-17s
	Group marking: W in a triangle
	Code letters: 600th Bomb Sqn 'N8-', 601st BS '3O-', 602nd BS 'K8-', 603rd BS 'N7-'
Afterwards:	To RAF Jul 1945, to care and maintenance and closed 1959

THE 55th Fghter Group's P-38H and 'J Lightnings offered early long-range escort to the Eighth Air Force Bomber steams until the P-51D Mustangs took on the role. The 55th moved in from Nuthampstead in April 1944 and was the first USAAF fighter unit to fly over Berlin. After this the P-38s adopted a tactical role. The Fortresses of the 398th settled in during April 1944, pulling out in June 1945 but still managing 195 operational missions in that time.

OLD BUCKENHAM, Norfolk

Station:	144
Location:	South east of Attleborough, east of the B1077 and north of the village of Old Buckenham
Previously:	Built for the USAAF, Oct 1942
Major Units:	Eighth Air Force, 453rd Bomb Group – B-24s
	Group markings: J in a circle
	Code letters: 732nd Bomb Sqn 'E3-', 733rd BS 'F8-', 734th BS 'E8-', 735th BS 'H6-'
Afterwards:	To the RAF, as a maintenance unit from May 1945 – with gaps to early 1958

OPERATING B-24Hs and 'Js, the 453rd received a lot of attention from March 1944 when a new Executive Officer ('XO') arrived for the 453rd, this was film actor James Stewart, who settled into his war role with seriousness and determination. The USAAF flew its last mission in April 1945 and had gone without trace by the summer. Today there is a superb and welcoming recreational flying facility.

Masking up the tail of a B-17 at Podington ready for the 92nd Bomb Group's 'B in a Triangle' marking and individual code letter. US NATIONAL ARCHIVES

PODINGTON, Bedfordshire

Station:	109
Location:	South of Rushden, west of Sharnbrook, signed off the A6
Previously:	RAF from Aug 1942 as satellite of Chelveston. USAAF from Apr 1943
Major Units:	Eighth Air Force, **92nd Bomb Group**, 'Fame's Favored Few' – B-17s Group markings: B in a triangle Code letters: 325th Bomb Sqn 'NV-', 326th BS 'JW-', 327th BS 'UX-', 407th BS 'PY-'
Afterwards:	Closed in 1946. To agriculture and – from the early 1960s the Santa Pod Raceway

BEFORE THE arrival of the B-17Fs and later 'Gs of 'Fame's Favored Few' – the 92nd BG – Podington saw varied use from April 1943, including brief sojourns by photo-recce units, a crew readiness section and temporarily 'homeless' bomb squadrons. The 92nd was very active at 'Pod' from September 1943 before moving on to France in June 1945. The airfield was closed by early 1946 and reverted to agriculture. It became the home of the Santa Pod Raceway drag racing strip in the early 1960s and remains so. The rubber burnt today is still using concrete laid down for a very different form of acceleration.

Memorial to 'Fame's Favored Few' – the 92nd Bomb Group – at Podington. KEN ELLIS

POLEBROOK, Northamptonshire

Station:	110
Location:	East of Oundle and the A605
Previously:	RAF from Sep 1940. Home to 90 Squadron and its Fortress Is
Major Units:	Eighth Air Force, **97th Bomb Group** – B-17s 340th, 341st, 342nd and 414th Bomb Squadrons – no code letters or group markings Eighth Air Force, **351st Bomb Group** – B-17s Group markings: J in a triangle Code letters: 508th Bomb Sqn 'YB-', 509th BS 'RQ-', 510th BS 'TU-', 511th BS 'DS-'
Afterwards:	Returned to RAF Jul 1945, closed 1948. Now an industrial estate

THE 97th Bomb Group flew the USAAF Eighth Air Force's first heavy bomber mission on August 17, 1942, from Polebrook. The unit operated B-17Es and later 'Fs, before moving to Grafton Underwood in November 1942. The 351st, with B-17Fs and later 'Gs, had the longest tenure at Polebrook, flying 311 missions, between May 1943 and Jun 1945.

Disbelieving aircrew examine flak damage to the starboard rear fuselage of a Polebrook-based 351st Bomb Group B-17. US NATIONAL ARCHIVES

PRESTWICK, Scotland

Location:	North west of Ayr and Prestwick, to the west of the A77
Previously:	RAF throughout. First USAAF use Jul 1942
Major Units:	Air Transport Command
Afterwards:	Last USAAF operations Sep 1945. See below for post-war usage

FAMED AS the main eastern element of the Atlantic Ferry Organisation, the USAAF used Prestwick extensively as a terminal for ferry flights bringing aircraft to the UK and beyond, and as a base for ATC Douglas C-54 Skymasters plying the Atlantic.

The heavy transports of the USAF's Military Air Transport Service (MATS) returned in 1951 – a terminal was set up and the runway lengthened. MATS became Military Airlift Command in 1966 and Prestwick continued its role alongside increasing airline usage and the aircraft production of Scottish Aviation. Resident from the early 1950s was the 67th Air Rescue Squadron (renamed the 57th ARS in June 1960), which operated SB-29s, SC-54s, Grumman SA-16 Albatrosses and Sikorsky SH-19A Chickasaw helicopters from Prestwick until September 1966 when the USAF presence dwindled. Today Prestwick is a major airport, maintenance centre, an 'aerostructures' plant and home to a Fleet Air Arm Sea King helicopter detachment – the latter using the old ARS premises.

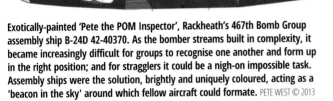

Exotically-painted 'Pete the POM Inspector', Rackheath's 467th Bomb Group assembly ship B-24D 42-40370. As the bomber streams built in complexity, it became increasingly difficult for groups to recognise one another and form up in the right position; and for stragglers it could be a nigh-on impossible task. Assembly ships were the solution, brightly and uniquely coloured, acting as a 'beacon in the sky' around which fellow aircraft could formate. PETE WEST © 2013

RACKHEATH, Norfolk

Station:	145
Location:	South east of the village of Rackheath, east of the A1161. Airfield lay west of the railway line
Previously:	Built for the USAAF, Nov 1943
Major Units:	Eighth Air Force, **467th Bomb Group** 'The Rackheath Aggies' – B-24s Group markings: P in a circle Code letters: 788th Bomb Sqn 'X7-', 789th BS '6A-', 790th BS 'Q2-', 791st BS '4Z-'
Afterwards:	To the RAF for maintenance unit usage from Jul 1945; reserve airfield from 1954. To agriculture by early 1960s

HOME TO the 'Rackheath Aggies', the 467th operated B-24Hs, 'Js, 'Ls and 'Ms on strategic, tactical and supply drop missions, from February 1944. Their major claim to fame was to be found on the 790th's dispersal, B-24H-15-FO 42-52534 *Witchcraft* with a 130 missions to her name without one abort once off the ground – a record for the 'Mighty Eighth'.

A section of Rackheath is now an industrial estate, but there are reminders of its previous use, including a memorial. BOTH KEN ELLIS

RAMSBURY, Wiltshire

Station:	469
Location:	North west of Hungerford, to the south west of the town
Previously:	USAAF from operational, Aug 1942
Major Units:	Ninth Air Force, **437th Troop Carrier Group** – C-47s, CG-4As and Airspeed Horsas Code letters: 83rd Troop Carrier Sqn 'T2-', 84th TCS 'Z8-', 85th TCS '9O-', 86th TCS '5K-'
Afterwards:	To RAF Feb 1945, flying stopped spring of 1946. Little of the airfield remains

THE 64th TCG moved in during August 1942 to get ready for Operation TORCH in North Africa and departed the following month. Ramsbury was not done with C-47s, however as the 437th TCG — glider-towing specialists – arrived in February 1944. After D-Day, it was again in action towing CG-4As for the Rhine Crossing in September 1944.

RATTLESDEN, Suffolk

Station:	126
Location:	South of the village of Rattlesden, south east of Felsham
Previously:	Built for the USAAF, 1942
Major Units:	Eighth Air Force, **322nd Bomb Group** – B-26Bs 447th Bomb Group – B-17s Group markings: K in a square Code letters: 708th Bomb Sqn 'CQ-', 709th BS 'IE-', 710th BS 'IJ-', 711th BS 'IR-'
Afterwards:	To the RAF Oct 1945, used for storage and in the 1960s Bloodhound SAM site. Light aircraft are based

THE B-26s of the 322nd, which co-located at Bury St Edmunds (Rougham), Suffolk, in June 1943, were the first of their type to fly operations from Britain. The B-17Gs of the 447th were based from November 1943 to August 1945. Much of the 'hardware' to be seen today is post-war RAF vintage.

RAYDON, Suffolk

Station:	157
Location:	North east of the village of Raydon, south of the A1071
Previously:	Built for the USAAF 1943
Major Units:	Eighth Air Force, **353rd Fighter Group** – P-47s and P-51s
	Code letters: 350th Fighter Sqn 'LH-', 351st FS 'YJ-', 352nd FS 'SX-'
Afterwards:	To the RAF 1946, non-flying use, disposed of in 1958. Northern edge of the former airfield is home to light aircraft based

PRIOR TO the 353rd Fighter Group arriving at Raydon, the Ninth Air Force was present briefly in the form of the 357th FG operating P-51Bs in late 1943, followed by the 358th FG with P-47Ds in late January 1944 to early March 1944. The 353rd flew P-47s from April 1944 and P-51Ds from October 1944 to October 1945. Much of the wartime airfield, including a pair of T2 hangars, can still be seen.

Bill Price, then Captain, with h P-51D 'Janie' Raydon, 194 US NATIONAL ARCHIV

Two pilots (centre) and groundcrew with P-51D 'Alabama Rammer Jammer' of the Raydon-based 352nd Fighter Squadron. The pilot on the right is 'packing' a Colt 45 in a shoulder holster. US NATIONAL ARCHIVES

RIDGEWELL, Essex

Station:	167
Location:	South of Clare, north east of the village of Ridgewell
Previously:	RAF from November 1942
Major Units:	Eighth Air Force, **381st Bomb Group** – B-17s
	Group markings: L in a triangle
	Code letters: 532nd Bomb Sqn 'VE-', 533rd BS 'VP-', 534th BS 'GD-', 535th BS 'MS-'
Afterwards:	To RAF July 1945, non-flying usage. USAF storage base 1960-1967

PROUD WINNER of two Distinguished Unit Citations, the 381st operated from Ridgewell from June 1943 using initially B-17Fs and then B-17Gs. The 381st took the highest losses in the infamous Schweinfurt raid of August 1943. Today part of the airfield is used for gliding, but the bulk has returned to agriculture.

Established in what was Station 167's hospital is the **Ridgewell Airfield Commemorative Museum** and the **381st Bomb Group Memorial Museum** with a wealth of material. Open the second Sunday of each month, April to September. More details: 07543 658006 **www.381st.com**

Lt Col J J Nazarro (right), CO of Ridgewell's 381st Bomb Group, greeting Brig Gen Robert B Williams, head of the 1st Air Division. KEC

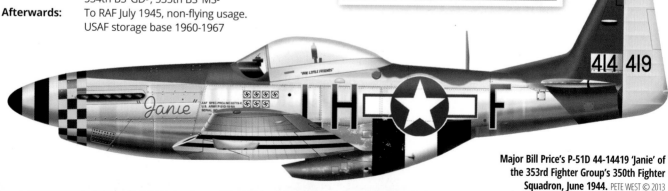

Major Bill Price's P-51D 44-14419 'Janie' of the 353rd Fighter Group's 350th Fighter Squadron, June 1944. PETE WEST © 2013

B-17G 42-31075 'The Rebel' of the 535th Bomb Squadron, 381st BW, Ridgewell. PETE WEST © 2013

B-17s of the 381st Bomb Group taxying out at Ridgewell. US NATIONAL ARCHIVES

The 381st Bomb Group's 'L in a Triangle' markings compromising the camouflage of a 535th BS example. US NATIONAL ARCHIVES

Personnel gathered around Ridgewell's tower. In the foreground is the signal square providing runway and circuit information and the all-important 'RD' airfield identifier. KEC

Hangar space was always at a premium on a bomber base and crews worked outside in all weathers. Wright R-1820s presumably undergoing salvage with a 381st B-17G in the background. Note the bicycles – vital fast communication devices! US NATIONAL ARCHIVES

'Sugar', B-17G 42-37721 of the 381st's 534th Bomb Squadron after salvage following a failure of the starboard undercarriage. US NATIONAL ARCHIVES

B-26 Marauders of the Rivenhall-based 397th Bomb Group. In the foreground are examples from the 597th Bomb Squadron, while below are ones from the 598th. US NATIONAL ARCHIVES

RIVENHALL, Essex

Station:	168
Location:	North of Witham and the A12, north east of Silver End
Previously:	USAAF from operational, Jan 1944
Major Units:	Ninth Air Force, **397th Bomb Group** – B-26s Code letters: 596th Bomb Sqn 'X2-', 597th BS '9F-', 598th BS 'U2-', 599th BS '6B-'
Afterwards:	To RAF Oct 1944. Flying ceased Jan 1946

RIVENHALL BRIEFLY hosted the 363rd FG with P-51Ds from February to April 1944, moving on to Staplehurst, Kent. Like many other Essex airfields, it became a Marauder base, pounding tactical targets to support the Allied advance. The B-26s of the 397th relocated to Hurn, Dorset, in August 1944.

Rivenhall, looking eastwards: the 'spectacle' dispersals in the foreground were once crowded with Marauders. KEY

C-47 'E5-S' of the 314th Troop Carrier Group's 62nd Troop Carrier Squadron, based at Saltby. KEC

SALTBY, Leicestershire

Station:	538
Location:	North of Buckminster, east of the village of Saltby
Previously:	RAF from Aug 1941
Major Units:	Ninth Air Force, **314th Troop Carrier Group**, C-47s, C-53s, Waco CG-4s Code letters: 32nd Troop Carrier Sqn 'S2-', 50th TCS '2R-', 61st TCS 'Q9-', 62nd TCS 'E5-'
Afterwards:	Returned to the RAF Mar 1945, sold off in 1955

TODAY, SALTBY is the home of the Buckminster Gliding Club, an appropriate use for an airfield that once witnessed C-47s tugging Airspeed Horsas and CG-4As into the air. The 314th Troop Carrier Group, which arrived in February 1944, also operated C-53s and a handful of Consolidated C-109 Liberators from Saltby. The unit took part in D-Day and every airborne operation thereafter, moving to Poix in France in March 1945. Another Ninth Air Force unit was a lodger in May 1945, the 349th TCG operating Curtiss C-46 Commandos.

SCAMPTON, Lincolnshire

Location:	North of Lincoln, west of the A15
Previously:	RFC/RAF (when the airfield was known as Brattleby) Nov 1916 to 1920. RAF from Aug 1936
Major Units:	USAF SAC Jul 1948 to Feb 1949 – see below
Afterwards:	To the RAF Feb 1949. Currently home to the 'Red Arrows'

SCAMPTON HAD a brief period as an Strategic Air Command 'Cold War' forward bomber base with Boeing B-29 Superfortresses of the 28th Bomb Group and then the 301st BG was based here in 1948 to 1949.

SCORTON, Yorkshire

Station:	425
Location:	South east of Scotch Corner on the A1, west of the village of Scorton
Previously:	RAF from Oct 1939
Major Units:	Ninth Air Force, 422nd Night Fighter Squadron, May to Jul 1944, then 425th NFS Jun to Aug 1944
Afterwards:	Returned to the RAF Jul 1944. Closed by 1947

SCORTON WAS the only Yorkshire USAAF base, and Station 425 was graced by the incredible Northrop P-61 Black Widows of two independent squadrons, the 422nd and 425th NFSs both of which moved on to France with the tide of war. The Black Widows worked up in the night-fighter role but during D-Day were used for night intruder strike.

SCULTHORPE, Norfolk

Location:	West of Fakenham and Sculthorpe, north of the A148
Previously:	Built for the RAF early 1943, extensive use. Closed mid-1945
Major Units:	Major use from Jan 1949 by the USAF – see below
Afterwards:	Still an MoD site and occasionally used for exercises

STRATEGIC AIR Command started regular deployments to this extensive base from January 1949. Deployments from the USA of Boeing B-29 Superfortresses, B-50 Superfortresses and KB-29 tankers were frequently to be seen up to the mid-1950s. In support of this activity, the 9th Air Rescue Squadron (ARS) and later the

Saltby's memorial carries the flags of Poland, the UK and the USA. KEN ELLIS

567th ARS operated GSA-16 Albatrosses and SB-29s from the base up to the late 1950s. From 1951 the base became home to RB-45C Tornados of the 91st Strategic Reconnaissance Group used for long-ranging 'spook' flights into the 'Iron Curtain' and some of these flights were RAF-crewed. Further Tornados, this time bomber B-45As of the 47th Bomb Group, arrived in 1952, staying until 1956 when the unit replaced them with B-66 Destroyers which were used until 1962. From 1954, the 19th Tactical Reconnaissance Squadron arrived with RB-45Cs and operated alongside the 91st and then in their place until 1959. The 19th took on RB-66s in 1958 and flew them until 1962. By the mid-1960s, Sculthorpe was a storage site for the USAF and it was used as a dispersal base for exercises and other flights. This included Lockheed U-2C spyplanes in the mid-1970s. During the late 1970s and early 1980s, the base was home to large numbers of North American F-100 Super Sabres, Lockheed T-33As and Dassault Mystères surplus from the French Air Force and USAF funded. Many of these found their way into UK museums.

Fuel-hauling transport version of the B-24 Liberator, a C-109 of the 32nd Troop Carrier Squadron, Saltby. KEC

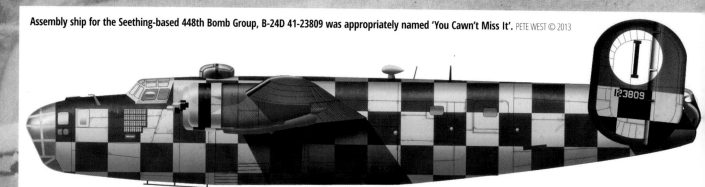

Assembly ship for the Seething-based 448th Bomb Group, B-24D 41-23809 was appropriately named 'You Cawn't Miss It'. PETE WEST © 2013

SEETHING, Norfolk

Station:	146
Location:	North of Bungay, east of the B1332 and south of the village of Seething
Previously:	Built for the USAAF, Mar 1943
Major Units:	Eighth Air Force, **448th Bomb Group** – B-24s
	Group markings: I in a circle
	Code letters: 712th Bomb Sqn 'CT-', 713th BS 'IG-', 714th BS 'EI-', 715th BS 'IO-'
Afterwards:	To the RAF, for maintenance unit use Jul 1945. Returned to agriculture in 1946

THE WAVENEY Flying Group operates from a part of the 448th's former airfield, keeping the memories going. Today light aircraft fly where once there were mighty B-24Hs, 'Js, 'Ls and 'Ms, from December 1943 to July 1945.

The original control tower has been restored as the **Station 146 Control Tower Museum** and serves as a living memorial to the 448th Bomb Group. The brochure and website sum it up well: "One building: a whole airfield of memories". Open first Sunday of May to October. More details: **www.seethingtower.org**

SHEPHERD'S GROVE, Suffolk

Location:	South east of Stanton, south of A143
Previously:	RAF from 1944, bomber training and then Central Signals Establishment. To care and maintenance 1950
Major Units:	See below
Afterwards:	Returned to the RAF 1959 Thor IRBM site up to 1963. USAF support and domestic site well into the 1970s

IN EARLY 1951 a USAF working party came to Shepherd's Grove to get the base ready to take the 81st Fighter Interceptor Wing equipped with F-86A Sabres. The FIW arrived in August and comprised the 92nd and 116th (later re-numbered the 78th) FISs. From April 1954 the 81st changed role from interceptor to tactical strike – including the delivery of 'special weapons' – atomic bombs. Fully operational with F-84F Thunderstreaks from February 1955, the 81st Fighter Bomber Wing kept one squadron at the 'Grove, the 78th FBS. From mid-1958 the unit again changed designation, becoming the 81st Tactical Fighter Wing which moved on to Woodbridge, also Suffolk, that December when the base was returned to the RAF. Many buildings remain today, in use for light industry and other purposes.

B-24s and a couple of C-47s in the dispersals at Shipdham. KEC

B-24s of the 68th Bomb Squadron, 44th Bomb Group, en route to a target. KEC

INSET: A 44th Bomb Group Pathfinder B-24 with its munitions annotated. US NATIONAL ARCHIVES

SHIPDHAM, Norfolk

Station:	115
Location:	East of the village of Shipdham and the A1075, north of Letton Green
Previously:	Built for the USAAF, May 1942
Major Units:	Eighth Air Force, **44th Bomb Group** 'The Flying Eightballs' – B-24s Group marking: A in a circle Code letters: 66th Bomb Sqn 'QK-', 67th BS 'NB-', 68th BS 'WQ-', 506th BS 'GJ-'
Afterwards:	To RAF for maintenance unit use Apr 1946 to Dec 1947 then to agriculture

THE 44th Bomb Group was the first USAAF unit with Liberators and its B-24Ds took the brunt of the Eighth Air Force's learning curve with the Liberator as a weapon of war. The 44th was deployed to North Africa twice during its stay at Shipdham, the first time from June to August 1943 to Libya for the famous Ploesti raid. The unit, known as 'The Flying Eightballs', received two Distinguished Unit Citations for its exploits. In the 1970s the western side of the airfield re-opened for light aviation and, under the Shipdham Aero Club, continues to thrive.

SNAILWELL, Suffolk

Station:	361
Location:	North of Newmarket and south east of the village. The A14 cuts through the southern boundary of the airfield
Previously:	RAF from spring 1941 – extensive use
Major Units:	See below
Afterwards:	Returned to the RAF autumn 1944. Closed in 1946. Little remains today

SNAILWELL HAD fleeting USAAF usage, but provided a vital support role for the Ninth Air Force's tactical units. From May 1944 the 33rd and 41st Mobile Repair and Reclamation Squadrons and the 51st Service Squadron were resident, specialising in the overhaul and repair of A-20G Havocs with great emphasis on the build-up to D-Day and sustaining the move into France.

SNETTERTON HEATH, Norfolk

Station:	138
Location:	South west of Attleborough, south of Snetterton and the A11
Previously:	Built for the USAAF, Nov 1942
Major Units:	Eighth Air Force, **96th Bomb Group** – B-17s Group markings: C in a square Code letters: 337th Bomb Sqn 'AW-', 338th BS 'BX-', 339th BS 'QJ-', 413th BS 'MZ-'
Afterwards:	To the RAF for maintenance unit usage, Dec 1945, sold off early 1960s.

THE AIRFIELD is now home to the Snetterton motor racing circuit and much of the layout of the B-17 base can still be appreciated. The 96th BG arrived in June 1943 with B-17Fs and stayed unusually late following the end of the war in Europe – December 1945 – with B-17Gs. As a group it suffered badly, with 189 aircraft failing to return.

Fire Brigade

DANGER EXHAUST

During the 1960s and early 1970s, major USAF bases had a detachment of the 40th Air Rescue and Recovery Wing on standby in case of a downed aircraft. Equipped with the amazing-looking Kaman HH-43B Huskie, crews were on immediate standby to airlift fire fighters, or rescue equipment, to the scene. Injured aircrew could be placed on stretchers and loaded through the clam-shell doors at the rear of the helicopter. The HH-43 had twin rotors that intermeshed, as can be seen in this dramatic **image.** USAF-KEC

SUBSCRIBERS CALL FOR YOUR **SPECIALS' DISCOUNT**

£4.99 INC FREE P&P*

£7.99 INC FREE P&P*

£4.99 INC FREE P&P*

£7.99 INC FREE P&P*

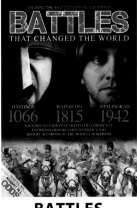

RAF 2013
Behind the scenes insight into the aircraft, equipment and people of one of the world's premier air forces

132 **PAGES**

BATTLES
A unique look at three major battles from world history, with specially commissioned images and in-depth maps

100 **PAGES**

US NAVY AIRPOWER
Dedicated to the US Navy's air operations from around the world, with reviews of 12 months of operations by the US Navy's Carrier Air Wings.

100 **PAGES**

MOST EXCLUSIVE
A small number of wealthy businessmen and enthusiast groups who acquired former main line locomotives for their own use.

132 **PAGES**

£4.99 INC FREE P&P*

£4.99 INC FREE P&P*

£4.99 INC FREE P&P*

£4.99 INC FREE P&P*

SCALE MODELLING
Sage advice for beginners, those returning to the hobby & even more experienced modelers. It's everything you need to know to produce a great model

100 **PAGES**

RAF SALUTE 2010
A unique blending of the history of the RAF and its present-day capabilities, topics from the first UK Jet to the last of the Spitfires.

100 **PAGES**

AIRLINER CLASSICS 4
The latest edition of the tribute to the classic years of aviation. Featuring Concorde & British Eagle

100 **PAGES**

SPACE
The complete story of humankind's incredible efforts to break the bonds of Earth.

100 **PAGES**

MAGAZINE SPECIALS

ESSENTIAL reading from the teams behind your **FAVOURITE** magazines

HOW TO **ORDER**

VISIT

www.keypublishing.com/shop

OR

PHONE
UK: 01780 480404
ROW: (+44)1780 480404

NEW FREE Aviation Specials App

KEY

Simply download to purchase digital versions of your favourite aviation specials in one handy place! Once you have the app, you will be able to download new, out of print or archive specials for less than the cover price!

IN APP ISSUES £3.99

*Free 2nd class P&P on all UK & BFPO orders. Overseas charges apply. Postage charges vary depending on total order value.

159/13

Bombing up B-26 Marauders of the 344th Bomb Group at Stansted in 1944. GEORGE KAMMERMEYER VIA WARREN E THOMPSON

SPANHOE, Northamptonshire

Station	493
Location:	South west of Duddington, west of the A43 and east of Harringworth village
Previously:	Built for the USAAF, late 1943
Major Units:	Ninth Air Force, **315th Troop Carrier Group** – C-47s, C-53s and see below
	Code letters: 34th Troop Carrier Sqn 'NM-', 43rd TCS 'UA-', 309th TCS 'M6-', 310th TCS '4A-'
Afterwards:	To the RAF – storage site – May 1945 and closed 1947

THE 315th Troop Carrier Group arrived in February 1944 and was involved in every airborne operation through to the end of the war. The 315th operated a variety of types: C-47s, C-53s, C-109s, Horsas, CG-4As, Airspeed Oxfords and Piper L-4 Grasshoppers. The unit moved out to Amiens in France in May 1945. Today a part of the southern taxi track serves as the runway for a thriving light aircraft population and is the home to Windmill Aviation, restoration and maintenance wizards.

Buildings in and around the former Motor Transport Wing survive at Spanhoe. KEN ELLIS

STANSTED, Essex

Station:	169
Location:	North east of Bishop's Stortford, east of the M11 and north of the A120
Previously:	USAAF from operational, May 1943
Major Units:	Ninth Air Force, **344th Bomb Group** – B-26s
	Code letters: 494th Bomb Sqn 'K9-', 495th BS 'Y5-', 496th BS 'N3-', 497th BS '7I-'
Afterwards:	See below

IT IS very hard these days to find any structures that relate to London Stansted Airport's USAAF origins. The airfield became host to the 30th Air Depot Group in May 1943, and specialised in outfitting newly-delivered B-26s among other support tasks. The B-26s of the 344th BG also arrived, moving on to Cormeilles-en-Vexin, France, in September 1944. The Air Depot was closed by June 1945. From 1946 there was a joint RAF/civilian presence. In October 1952 the USAF arrived, with Stansted becoming host to a variety of Air Base Squadrons in support of the Military Air Transport Service and Strategic Air Command. The east-west runway was massively extended, thereby helping to determine the airfield's later role. The USAF moved out in 1958 and Stansted became exclusively civil.

How many Stansted passengers realise the airspace was once dominated by Marauders? KEY

STAPLEHURST, Kent

Station:	413
Location:	Between Staplehurst and Headcorn, just south of the Tonbridge to Ashford railway line
Previously:	RAF ALG from Aug 1943
Major Units:	Ninth Air Force, **363rd Fighter Group** – P-51s Code letters: 380th Fighter Sqn 'A9-', 381st FS 'B3-', 382nd FS 'C3-'
Afterwards:	To farmland Oct 1944

THE 363RD's P-51Ds moved in from Rivenhall, Essex, in April 1944 but were initially allocated to bomber escort, only moving to tactical work during June. They departed in July, for Maupertus in France.

STONEY CROSS, Hampshire

Station	452
Location:	North west of Stoney Cross and Minstead, north of the A31 close to Junction 1 of the M27
Previously:	RAF from Nov 1942
Major Units:	Ninth Air Force, **367th Fighter Group** – P-38s Code letters: 392nd Fighter Sqn 'H5-', 393rd FS '8L-', 394th FS '4N-' Eighth Air Force, **387th Bomb Group** – B-26s Code letters: 556th Bomb Sqn 'FW-', 557th BS 'KS-', 558th BS 'KX-', 559th BS 'TQ-'
Afterwards:	To RAF Oct 1944, to care and maintenance 1946, to the Forestry Commission 1956

Mustang 'Sunny VIII', the personal mount of Colonel Everett Stewart, CO of the 4th Fighter Group. Stewart finished his tour with nine 'kills'.
BILL HESS VIA WARREN E THOMPSON

STEEPLE MORDEN, Cambridgeshire

Station:	122
Location:	North west of Royston, east of the village
Previously:	RAF from Jun 1940, satellite of Bassingbourn. USAAF from Oct 1942
Major Units:	Eighth Air Force, **355th Fighter Group** – P-47s and P-51s Code letters: 354th Fighter Squadron 'WR-', 357th FS 'OS-', 358th FS 'YF-'
Afterwards:	Closed as an airfield in Mar 1946, little traces of its heritage left

STATION 122 saw limited USAAF use from opening and even co-hosted RAF bomber training 'ops' for a short while. From September 1943 the 355th Fighter Group was equipped with Republic P-47 Thunderbolts, but took on North American P-51B Mustangs in mid-1944, then gravitated to P-51Ds and 'Ks.

The 355th had the top aircraft 'kill' tally of the Eighth, in air-to-ground strafes. It received a Distinguished Unit Citation for an attack on a German airfield on April 5, 1944.

The famous red-nosed 4th Fighter Group - 'The Eagles' - moved into from Debden when the Essex base was returned to the RAF. The 4th Finally departed to the USA in November 1945, one of the last Fighter Groups to depart.

THE 367TH's P-38 Lightnings worked up at Stoney Cross directly after arriving from the USA and then went into the flak suppression and interdiction role before moving very briefly through Ibsley to Beuzeville, France. The P-38s were followed by the B-26s of the 387th moving in from Chipping Ongar, Essex in July 1944. They crossed the Channel to Maupertus in September 1944.

STURGATE, Lincolnshire

Location:	South east of Gainsborough, south of the village of Heapham
Previously:	RAF from 1944 to Jan 1946
Major Units:	See below
Afterwards:	To civil use 1965 onwards

UNDER OPERATION GALLOPER, Sturgate was home to Republic F-84F Thunderstreaks of Strategic Air Command's 27th (Strategic) Fighter Wing which were capable of wielding atomic weapons in a 'toss bombing' manoeuvre. Allocated to the USAF in July 1952, the base was activated in June 1953 and was home to an element of the SAC's 7th Air Division as a forward base. It saw fits and starts of operational use until 1964. Today the airfield is used for general aviation.

SUDBURY, Suffolk

Station:	174
Location:	North east of Sudbury, north of the B1115, west of Great Waldingfield
Previously:	Built for the USAAF 1944
Major Units:	Eighth Air Force, **486th Bomb Group** – B-24s and B-17s
	Group markings: O in a square
	Code letters: 832nd Bomb Sqn '3R-', 833rd BS '4N-', 834th BS '2S-', 835th BS 'H8-'
Afterwards:	Returned to the RAF summer of 1945, held in care and maintenance. Closed late 1950s.

EQUIPPED WITH B-24Hs and B-24Js between March 1944 to July 1944 and then B-17Gs to August 1945, the 486th undertook 188 missions from Sudbury. Redevelopment started in 1952 in readiness for the USAF, but this was not completed and the work halted in 1955. Much of the airfield structure and layout can be seen today.

The tower at Station 174, Sudbury, 1944. KEC

THORPE ABBOTTS, Norfolk

Station:	139
Location:	East of Diss, between the A140 and the A143, north of the village of Thorpe Abbotts
Previously:	Built for the USAAF, Apr 1943
Major Units:	Eighth Air Force, **100th Bomb Group** 'The Bloody Hundredth' – B-17s
	Group markings: D in a square
	Code letters: 349th Bomb Sqn 'XR-', 350th BS 'LN-', 351st BS 'EP-', 418th BS 'LD-'
Afterwards:	To the RAF Jun 1945, used as 'Standby Airfield' and then to care and maintenance. Closed in the mid-1950s

THE 100th BG got its nickname 'The Bloody Hundredth' for the worst of reasons, the unit endured periods of utter carnage, ending up with 177 aircraft missing in action. Two Distinguished Unit Citations marked the unit's valour. The KC-135 tankers of the 100th Air Refueling Wing, based at

The flying wires of a Tiger Moth frame the tower and buildings that form the evocative 100th Bomb Group Memorial Museum. KEN ELLIS

Mildenhall in Suffolk, still carry the famous D in a square marking in commemoration of the 100th BG's Boeings of another era.

The **100th Bomb Group Memorial Museum** offers poignant insights into the life and times of the men and machines of the 'Bloody Hundredth' inside the original control tower and other wartime buildings. 'Brown signed' from the A140 and the A143 it is open March to October at weekends and Bank Holidays, and stages regular special events. More: 01379 740708 **www.100bgmus.org.uk**

Well-known, but nevertheless fabulous, photo of a 351st Bomb Squadron B-17G amid the winter snow of 1944 at Thorpe Abbotts. US NATIONAL ARCHIVES

Northampton's Tribute

There is much on the legacy of the USAAF in Northamptonshire to be found within the Sywell Aviation Museum. KEN ELLIS

★ The USAAF was very active in Northamptonshire, and the Sywell Aviation Museum at Northampton's delightful Sywell aerodrome charts this heritage comprehensively. The museum, which contains much else to fascinate, is 'guarded' by the only complete surviving Hawker Hunter F.2, and the car park doubles as a viewing area for the aerodrome. Open weekends and Bank Holidays from Easter to the end of September. More details: **www.sywellaerodrome.co.uk/museum.php**

Post-war Thurleigh became home to the Royal Aircraft Establishment but now is the domain of motor transport and high-performance cars. KEY

THURLEIGH, Bedfordshire

Station:	111
Location:	North of Bedford, north of the village
Previously:	RAF from Jul 1941 – bomber training. USAAF from Sep 1942
Major Units:	Eighth Air Force, **306th Bomb Group** 'The Reich Wreckers' – B-17s Group markings: H in a triangle Code letters: 367th Bomb Sqn 'GY-', 368th BS 'BO-', 369th BS 'WW-', 423rd BS 'RD-'
Afterwards:	To RAF 1946 and airfield massively modified to become Royal Aircraft Establishment Bedford, huge single runway, wind tunnels etc. Closed in March 1994, although wind tunnel site is still operating. Rest of airfield motor racing trials and experience course – 'Bedford Autodrome'

The red tail fin tip and spinners denote a B-17G of the 367th Bomb Squadron of Thurleigh's 306th Bomb Group. BEN MARCILONIS VIA WARREN E THOMPSON

The 306th Bomb Group Museum at Thurleigh has turned the former Small Arms and Ammunition Store into a shrine to the 'Reich Wreckers'. KEY-KEN ELLIS

THE B-17Fs and 'Gs of 'The Reich Wreckers' held the longest tenure of any Eighth Air Force Bomb Group in the UK. The unit arrived in September 1942 and remained loyal to the same base by virtue of its stay-over post-war awaiting transfer into Germany as part of the occupying forces in November 1945. RAE became the Defence Science and Technology Laboratory in the 1990s and some of the wind tunnel complex continues to function.

The **306th Bomb Group Museum**, located in the wartime Small Arms and Ammunition Store, is an absorbing and loving tribute to 'The Reich Wreckers'. Open weekends and Bank Holidays, March to October. More details: 01234 708715 **www.306bg.co.uk**

THRUXTON, Hampshire

Station:	407
Location:	North of the A303, west of Andover, Hampshire
Previously:	RAF from Jun 1941
Major Units:	Ninth Air Force, **366th Fighter Group** – P-47s Code letters: 389th Fighter Sqn 'A6-', 390th FS 'B2-', 391st FS 'A8-'
Afterwards:	To RAF Jul 1944, sold off 1946. Currently a thriving general aviation airfield and motor racing circuit

THRUXTON BECAME a US base in March 1944 and is another with a familiar pattern, the Thunderbolts of the 366th established themselves at Membury, Berkshire, before moving closer to the action at Thruxton in April 1944 until they could move to the Continent – St Pierre de Mont, France – in mid-June 1944.

TIBENHAM, Norfolk

Station: 124
Location: North of the B1134, between Gissing Common and Tibenham
Previously: Built for the USAAF, Jun 1943
Major Units: Eighth Air Force, **445th Bomb Group** – B-24s
Group markings: F in a circle
Code letters: 700th Bomb Sqn 'IS-', 701st BS 'MK-', 702nd BS 'WV-', 703rd BS 'RN-'
Afterwards: To the RAF Jul 1945. Redeveloped in 1955 and with the USAF 1956-1957 for possible use. Closed 1959. Now in use for gliding

AT FIRST glance, visitors to Tibenham may think the base in a good state of repair, but much of the runways and other concrete that is visible is from extensions of the mid-1950s for possible use by the USAF. Operating B-24Hs, 'Js, 'Ls and 'Ms the 445th suffered horrific loses – all to the Luftwaffe – on a raid to Kassel on September 27, 1944 when 28 out of 37 B-24 despatched fell from the skies.

TOOME, Northern Ireland

Station: 236
Location: At the northern point of Lough Neagh, off the A6 between Magherafelt and Randalstown
Previously: RAF. Transferred to USAAF Jul 1942
Major Units: Combat Crew Replacement Center – 8th Composite Command
Afterwards: Returned to RAF Nov 1944. MU use only, closed 1947

WITH ATCHAM handling fighter acclimatisation training and Greencastle doing likewise for B-17 and B-24s crews, Toome did similar work for A-20 Havoc and B-26 Marauder crews. Oddly, the base remained an Eighth Air Force asset, even though the majority – and eventually all – of its trained personnel went on to fly with the Ninth Air Force. Much of the former airfield is still to be seen.

UPOTTERY, Devon

Station: 462
Location: North west of the A30/A303 and of Upottery village; close to Smeatharpe
Previously: USAAF from operational, Feb 1944
Major Units: Ninth Air Force, **439th Troop Carrier Group** – C-47s, C-53s and CG-4As
Code letters: 91st Troop Carrier Sqn 'L4-', 92nd TCS 'J8-', 93rd TCS '3B-', 94th TCS 'D8-'
US Navy VB-107 and VB-112 with PB4Y-1 Liberators
Afterwards: To RAF Jul 1945. Station closed Nov 1948. Fair amount still to be seen

AS WITH other TCGs within the South West, the 439th at Upottery worked up for D-Day, with the 101st Airborne as 'passengers'. The unit moved out to France in September 1944. In January, two US Navy Liberator squadrons arrived, hunting over the Bay of Biscay.

LEFT: **An Upper Heyford-based EF-111 Raven of the 42nd Electronic Countermeasures Squadron topping up from a Mildenhall KC-135. Ravens were a specially-modified ECM specialist version of the well-known 'sing-wing' F-111s that were stationed at Lakenheath, as well as Upper Heyford. The sophisticated F-111s gave the USAF spersonic, long-range strike capability.** KEY-DUNCAN CUBITT

UPPER HEYFORD, Oxfordshire

Location: North west of Bicester, north of the B4030, Oxfordshire
Previously: RAF from 1916 (with interruptions!). USAF from 1951
Major Units: See below
Afterwards: Base closed in 1994

A MAJOR rebuild of the former RAF station was initiated in 1950-1951 to ready it for a series of regular deployments of Boeing KB-29 tankers, B-50 and B-47 bombers and RB-36H strategic recce aircraft. From September 1966 Upper Heyford was home to the 66th Tactical Reconnaissance Wing, flying McDonnell RF-101 Voodoos and, from 1969, McDonnell Douglas RF-4C Phantoms. From 1970 the role changed dramatically, with the arrival of the 20th Tactical Fighter Wing with General Dynamics F-111 swing-wing bombers and from 1984 with the 'spook' EF-111 Ravens of the 42nd Electronic Countermeasures Squadron. All the F-111s had gone by 1992. Today the base is the expanding Heyford Park industrial, storage and technology park; within is a small museum, available for inspection by prior application only: **www.raf-upper-heyford.org**

WARMWELL, Dorset

Station: 454 – also known as Woodsford
Location: South east of Dorchester, Dorset
Previously: RAF since May 1937
Major Units: Ninth Air Force, **474th Fighter Group** – P-38s
Code letters: 428th Fighter Sqn 'F5-', 429th FS '7Y-', 430th FS 'K6-'
Afterwards: To the RAF August 1944, station closed October 1945. Little of the airfield can be seen today

AFTER BRIEF detachments of Spitfires (31st Fighter Group) in mid-1943 and P-47 Thunderbolts (4th FG) in September 1943, Warmwell was occupied by the long-ranging P-38s of the 474th FG from March 1944, ready to support D-Day. The unit moved to France in August 1944.

WARTON, Lancashire

Station: 582
Location: West of Preston, south of Warton and Freckleton on the shores of the River Ribble
Previously: No use prior to USAAF from Jun 1942
Major Units: 2nd Base Air Depot
Afterwards: Returned to RAF Nov 1945 – 90 Maintenance Unit until mid-1951

CLOSE TO the port of Liverpool and with a large labour pool available from Preston and area, Warton was short listed as a location for one of the massive BADs designed to support the huge influx of USAAF aircraft for the war effort. Nearly 3,000 B-24s were handled by the facility out of a grand total of 10,068 processed of 20 different types – the 2nd was the largest of the BADs.

The extensive facilities attracted English Electric post-war and the airfield was used for flight testing the prototype Canberra in May 1949. Since then, EE, later BAC and now BAE Systems, has turned the airfield into its major flight test and final assembly centre, today working on Tornado upgrades and production of the Eurofighter Typhoon.

Eagles

Warren E Thompson presents a portfolio on the men and machines of the 4th Fighter Group

'Triple ace' Colonel Donald J M Blakeslee was the 4th Fighter Group's CO January to November 1944 when it was based at Debden, Essex. Blakeslee joined the RAF and flew Spitfires with 133 'Eagle' Squadron at Debden, clocking up three 'kills' while was wearing a light blue uniform. When the 4th was set up at Debden on September 29, 1942 the three RAF 'Eagle' Squadrons, 71, 121 and 133 'slid across', changed uniforms and put 'stars n bars' on the Spitfires. Blakeslee went on to achieve 15.5 aerial victories with the 4th's 335th Fighter Squadron.
USAF VIA WARREN E THOMPSON

ABOVE: **Major Pierce McKinnon returning from a mission: he had 12 confirmed 'kills'. Behind is a 335th FS P-51B.** TOM IVIE VIA WARREN E THOMPSON

RIGHT: **The 4th Fighter Group was granted a Distinguished Unit Citation for the highest combined victory total: 189 air-to-air 'kills' and 134 enemy aircraft destroyed on the ground. This incredible total included 16.5 for Ralph K Hofer, who chalked up his maiden victory on his first mission with the 4th's 334th FS. He was killed in action over Yugoslavia in a 4th FG P-51D on July 2, 1944.** TOM IVIE VIA WARREN E THOMPSON

BELOW: **Major Fred W Glover was credited with 10.33 'kills' while flying P-51Bs and P-51Ds with the 4th.** TOM IVIE VIA WARREN E THOMPSON

Captain Don Gentile (left) with Major Duane W Beeson (171/3 'kills') alongside Don's 336th FS P-51B 'Shangri La'. For details of Gentile's career, see Debden in the 'A to Z' section. BILL HESS VIA WARREN E THOMPSON

Wattisham in 1944, looking north west, with P-51s and some P-38s parked out. Two of the 'C' Type hangars remain gutted from a Luftwaffe incendiary raid of 1941. KEC

WATTISHAM, Suffolk

Station	377
Location:	South west of Needham Market, north of the B1078
Previously:	RAF from Mar 1939, extensive usage to Sep 1942
Major Units:	See below for first major USAAF usage. Eighth Air Force, **479th Fighter Group** 'Riddle's Raiders' – P-38s and P-51s Code letters: 434th Fighter Sqn 'L2-', 435th FS 'J2-', 436th FS '9B-'
Afterwards:	To care and maintenance late 1945 followed by extensive RAF usage, up to Oct 1992 when last Phantom left. Since major Army Air Corps helicopter base

Major Robin Olds of the 479th Fighter Group, 1944. With the Eighth Air Force he notched up 12 'kills' and then became a legend flying F-4 Phantoms in Vietnam, with four more victories. DAVID BORN VIA WARREN E THOMPSON

A P-38J Lightning of the 479th Fighter Group getting airborne at Wattisham. KEC

WATTISHAM HAS had an incredible history – used by the RAF, USAAF and Army Air Corps, it remains a major front-line base. When the RAF pulled out in September 1942 Station 377 became home to the 3rd Advanced Air Depot and the 4th Strategic Air Depot, specialising in the maintenance of USAAF fighters and was constantly in the midst of frenetic activity. From April 1944 it was the home of the Lockheed P-38J Lightning-equipped 479th FG – 'Riddle's Raiders' – the last Eighth Air Force fighter unit to form up. It took its name from Col Kyle Riddle who led the unit until August 1944 when he was shot down. In his place came none other than Col Hubert Zemke, but he too was shot down in October. Riddle managed to evade capture and returned

ABOVE: **A P-47 inside the bombed-out No.2 Hangar at Wattisham: while there was no roof, it provided some shelter for the maintenance teams.** KEC

RIGHT: **Wattisham was an extensive RAF station prior to the USAAF taking it on. Post-war it expanded considerably.** PETE WEST © 2013

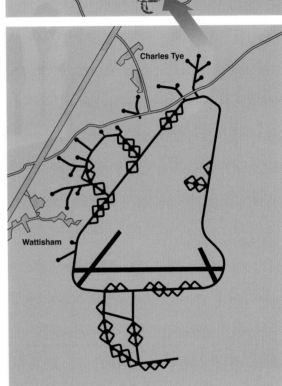

home to take over from the missing 'Hub' and led the 479th until the war's end. Among the Raiders' claims to fame was the air-to-air dispatch of a KG400 Messerschmitt Me 163 Komet on July 29, 1944, and it was the unit that shot down the Eighth's last enemy aircraft on April 24, 1945.

Wattisham Station Heritage, is run by the **Wattisham Museum Society** and is situated in what was the Station Chapel during the airfield's USAAF days. Displays are dedicated to every aspect of Wattisham's incredible history, from 1937 to date. As the airfield is an operational Army Air Corps base, visits have to be pre-booked; more details on: **www.wattishamairfieldmuseum.org**

Lt Arnold Helding of the 434th Fighter Squadron, on the wing of his bombed-up P-51D 'Lelah May' at Wattisham, 1945. KEC

A B-24J of the 392nd Bomb Group's 576th Bomb Squadron. KEY

WATTON, Norfolk

Station:	376
Location:	Just east of Watton, south of the B1108
Previously:	Built for the RAF, Mar 1939, extensive use
Major Units:	See below
Afterwards:	Returned to the RAF and used extensively. Flying (Canberras) ceased in 1969. Still largely MoD property

IN THE summer of 1943, Watton became an extensive facility to carry out deep maintenance, modifications and repair work to the USAAF's B-24s. This was the 3rd Strategic Air Depot. From April 1944 the 803rd Reconnaissance Group arrived operating modified B-17s and B-24s alongside de Havilland Mosquito PR.XVIs. The unit became the 15th BG (Reconnaissance) in August 1944. All USAAF presence had gone by June 1945.

WELFORD, Berkshire

Station	474
Location:	North west of Newbury, alongside the M4 motorway, Berks
Previously:	USAAF from operational, Sep 1943
Major Units:	Ninth Air Force, **438th Troop Carrier Gp** – C-47s Code letters: 87th Troop Carrier Sqn '3X-', 88th TCS 'M2-', 89th TCS '4U-', 90th TCS 'Q7-'
Afterwards:	To the RAF Jun 1945 and closed soon after. Re-opened as major US storage site (non-flying) 1955, out of use by 2002

THE 438th, which arrived in February 1944, used C-47s and tugged a mix of CG-4 Hadrian and Airspeed Horsas for D-Day and beyond. It moved to France in February 1945.

The **Ridgeway Military and Aviation Research Group** has an excellent museum within the site, now known as Welford Park. Visits are possible by prior arrangement only.

WENDLING, Norfolk

Station:	118
Location:	West of East Dereham, north of the A47 at Wendling and Hall Green
Previously:	Built for the USAAF, Jun 1943
Major Units:	Eighth Air Force, **392nd Bomb Group** 'The Crusaders' – B-24s Group markings: D in a circle Code letters: 576th Bomb Sqn 'CI-', 577th BS 'DC-', 578th BS 'EC-', 579th BS 'GC-'
Afterwards:	To the RAF Jun 1945 as a Standby airfield – little if any use. USAF communications site during the 1960s. Returned to agriculture

THE FIRST unit to take on the more capable and far better defended B-24H, the 392nd was involved in a wide series of bombing and support missions from Wendling. The unit went on to operate B-24Js, 'Ls and 'Ms and departed in June 1945.

RIGHT: **Weston Zoyland's classic three-runway layout. Today's A372 uses the main runway, dividing the site in two.** PETE WEST © 2013

WEST MALLING, Kent

Location:	South of West Malling, east of the A228 and north of Kent Street
Previously:	Civil from 1931, RAF from Mar 1940 to 1960
Major Units:	See below
Afterwards:	Small RAF enclave from mid-1960s plus varying civil aviation usage. Closed as airfield in early 1990s and now an industrial estate

WEST MALLING had a dazzling RAF career. It was used by the US Navy as a home for a communications unit from June 1960 when the R4D-8s moved in from Blackbushe, Hampshire. Later, Convair C-131F Samaritans were operated, prior to the unit settling into Mildenhall, Suffolk, in May 1964.

WESTON ZOYLAND, Somerset

Station:	447
Location:	East of Bridgwater, astride the A372
Previously:	RAF since 1926
Major Units:	Ninth Air Force, **442nd Troop Carrier Group** – C-47s, C-53s and CG-4s Code letters: 303rd Troop Carrier Sqn 'J7-', 304th TCS 'V4-', 305th TCS '4J-', 306th TCS '7H-'
Afterwards:	To RAF Oct 1944, closed 1946. Re-opened 1951 to Jan 1958

ANOTHER OF the units that took the 101st Airborne Division into battle on D-Day. The 442nd moved in during May 1944 and departed to France in October. Today the A372 cuts through the former airfield site, using the main runway as a foundation. Light aviation continues to use part of the site.

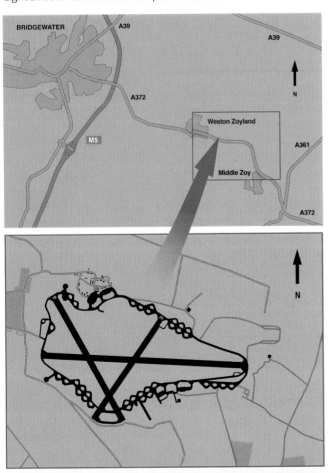

A-20 Havocs of the 668th Bomb Squadron, 446th Bomb Group over Le Havre on a mission out of Wethersfield. US NATIONAL ARCHVIES

WETHERSFIELD, Essex

Station:	170
Location:	West of Halstead, north of the village
Previously:	USAAF from operational, Feb 1944
Major Units:	Ninth Air Force, **416th Bomb Group** – A-20s Code letters: 668th Bomb Sqn '5H-', 669th BS '2A-', 670th BS 'F6-', 671st BS '5C-'
Afterwards:	See below

WETHERSFIELD SERVED the US military in two different eras. The 416th flew Douglas A-20G and 'H Havocs, particularly against V-1 flying-bomb sites. It moved forward in September 1944 to Melum-Villaroche, France. That month, the airfield was transferred to the RAF and it went into care and maintenance in early 1947.

In June 1951 it was allocated to the USAF as a fighter base and was extensively refurbished and enlarged. The 20th Fighter-Bomber Group, flying Republic F-84G Thunderjets arrived in May 1952. The unit was renamed the 20th Fighter-Bomber Wing in February 1955 and took on nuclear-capable Republic F-84F Thunderjets. In July 1957 significant re-equipment occurred with the arrival of North American F-100D and 'F Super Sabres of the 20th Tactical Fighter Wing. From 1957 it was home to the 23rd Helicopter Sqn, with H-21 Workhorses; changing to the 40th Air (later Aerospace) Rescue and Recovery Sqn in 1957 using HH-43 Huskies though to 1968. In mid-1970 the 20th started to relocate to Upper Heyford, Oxfordshire, in readiness for the General Dynamics F-111E. Wethersfield remained a significant Standby Operating Base and in the summer of 1975 was the centre of much attention as a detachment of Lockheed U-2Cs of the 100th Strategic Reconnaissance Wing operated from the airfield. By 1984 flying detachments were few and far between, and the USAF pulled out completely in late 1990. The airfield is now home to an RAF Volunteer Gliding School and also hosts some Ministry of Defence assets.

Fairchild A-10A Thunderbolt IIs of Woodbridge's 20th Tactical Fighter Wing. Fairchild took over Republic and named the A-10 in honour of the P-47. A-10s are known as 'Warthogs', from their good looks! KEY

WINKTON, Hampshire

Station	414
Location:	North east of Sopley and the B3347, south west of Bransgore
Previously:	RAF ALG from Sep 1943 – no usage
Major Units:	Ninth Air Force, 404th Fighter Group – P-47s Code letters: 506th Fighter Sqn '4K-', 507th FS 'Y8-', 508th FS '7J-'
Afterwards:	To farmland Mar 1945

THE 404th was particularly active during its brief time at Winkton, April to July 1944, establishing an exceptional record of ground-attack strikes, including attacking V-1 launch ramps.

WOODBRIDGE, Suffolk

Location:	South of the B1084, south east of Melton, within the Rendlesham Forest
Previously:	RAF from Sep 1943, extensive use as an emergency landing ground. Closed Mar 1948
Major Units:	See below
Afterwards:	Closed as a USAF base in 1993. Extensive buildings etc extant

WITH THE proximity to Bentwaters, Suffolk, Woodbridge was a good location for occupation by the USAF and extensive building work was carried out to achieve this. The 20th Fighter Bomber Wing arrived in mid-1952 flying F-84G Thunderjets, then F-84F Thunderstreaks and from 1957 F-100D Super Sabres. In 1969 the 20th converted to F-4D Phantom IIs and moved to Upper Heyford, Oxfordshire. The 81st Tactical Fighter Wing arrived from Shepherd's Grove in mid-1958 equipped initially with F-84Fs but later taking on the superlative F-101 Voodoo. In 1966 the 81st converted to F-4Cs and in 1977 – and an enlarged wing – took on the A-10A Thunderbolt II until disbanding in 1992. In November 1969 the 67th Aerospace Rescue and Recovery Squadron arrived from Spain with its C-130N and 'P Hercules and HH-3 'Jolly Green Giant' helicopters. In 1988 the HH-53Cs and 'Js 'Super Jollies' of the 21st Special Operations Squadron arrived. The 67th ARRS and the 21st SOS united to form the 67th Special Operations Group and moved base to Alconbury, Cambs. After all this activity, the base has an uneasy quiet about it, with much of the property being sold for industrial and storage use.

The P-47 flown by the 404th Fighter Group's CO, Colonel Carroll McColpin at Winkton.
ANDY WILSON VIA WARREN E THOMPSON

P-28 Lightnings of the 55th Fighter Group's 38th Fighter Squadron showing the transition from olive drab to natural metal.
US NATIONAL ARCHIVES

WOODCHURCH, Kent

Station	419
Location:	North of Woodchurch, west of Hengherst
Previously:	RAF Advanced Landing Ground from Jul 1943
Major Units:	Ninth Air Force, **373rd Fighter Group** – P-47s
	Code letters: 410th Fighter Sqn 'R3-', 411th 'U9-',
	412th FS 'V5-'
Afterwards:	To farmland Sep 1945

RAF AND Royal Canadian Air Force Mustangs used the Advanced Landing Ground before it was enlarged and remodelled for the USAAF P-47Ds, with the first Americans arriving in March 1944. The 373rd relocated to Tour-en-Bessin in France in July 1944.

WORMINGFORD, Essex

Station:	159
Location:	North east of Wakes Colne, south west of the village
Previously:	USAAF from operational, Nov 1943
Major Units:	Ninth Air Force, **362nd Fighter Group** – P-47s
	Code letters: 377th Fighter Sqn 'E4-', 378th FS 'G8-', 379th FS 'B8-'
	Eighth Air Force, **55th Fighter Group** – P-38s then P-51s
	Code letters: 38th Fighter Sqn 'CG-', 338th FS 'CL-', 334th FS 'CY-'
Afterwards:	USAAF left Jul 1945. To RAF that month, airfield closed Jan 1947. Currently agriculture with some gliding on site

The 362nd with its P-47Ds moved to Headcorn, Kent, in April 1944. Replacing it was the P-38J Lightning-equipped 55th from Nuthampstead, Herts, which used them for ground attack (often en masse) as well as escort duties. From July 1944 P-51Ds took over with P-51Ks joining them from December.

WYTON, Cambridgeshire

Location:	East of the A141, north west of St Ives
Previously:	RFC airfield 1916, closed in mid-1918. RAF from Oct 1935, mostly bombers. USAF from Nov 1950 to Mar 1952
Major Units:	See notes below
Afterwards:	To RAF Mar 1952 and used extensively by the RAF, becoming a centre for strategic photo-recce. Still RAF major station in admin and logistics, flying Air Cadets in Grob Tutors

WYTON BECAME a major rotational base for Strategic Air Command from November 1950, housing a series of temporary detachments from, in turn, the 93rd, 97th, 20th and 22nd BGs, all operating the Boeing B-50D much-modified Superfortress. B-29A and KB-29 tanker units were also to be found based. In the spring of 1952, the base returned to the RAF.

> **'Mighty Eighth'** is dedicated to all those personnel who have crossed the Atlantic to play their part in ridding the world of tyrants.

Down But Not Out

Second Lt William R Groseclose trusting the brakes on his P-51D Mustang 44-14431 'WD-Q' while posing with his crew chief for an 'action' publicity shot at Debden. Groseclose flew with the 4th Fighter Group's 335th Fighter Squadron during July to September 1944, completing 24 missions. His final sortie was on September 11th when he was involved in combat with a large number of Messerschmitt Bf 109s; he was shot down and parachuted to safety, becoming a prisoner of war. Undaunted he flew again with the 4th FG in Korea and also saw service in Vietnam, ending up as a Major. US NATIONAL ARCHIVES

The letter codes 'CG-' denote the 55th Fighter Group's 38th Fighter Squadron, in this case P-38H Lightning 'C-for-Charlie'. The 55th flew from Nuthampstead September 1943 to April 1944 then moved on to Wormingford. LOCKHEED

GROUP FINDER

Where was the 303rd based? What about the 91st? This guide will help you find the wartime base you want

GROUP	ROLE	AIRFIELD(S)
1st	FIGHTER	IBSLEY
4th	FIGHTER	DEBDEN, GREAT SAMPFORD
13th	PHOTO RECCE	MOUNT FARM
20th	FIGHTER	KING'S CLIFFE
31st	FIGHTER	ATCHAM, HIGH ERCALL
34th	BOMB	MENDLESHAM
36th	FIGHTER	KINGSNORTH
44th	BOMB	SHIPDHAM
48th	FIGHTER	IBSLEY
50th	FIGHTER	LYMINGTON
52nd	FIGHTER	EGLINTON, MEMBURY
55th	FIGHTER	NUTHAMPSTEAD, WORMINGFORD
56th	FIGHTER	BOXTED, HALESWORTH, HORSHAM ST FAITH
60th	TROOP CARRIER	ALDERMASTON
61st	TROOP CARRIER	BARKSTON HEATH
62nd	TROOP CARRIER	KEEVIL
67th	OBS / RECCE	MEMBURY, MIDDLE WALLOP
78th	FIGHTER	DUXFORD
81st	FIGHTER	HIGH ERCALL
91st	BOMB	BASSINGBOURN
92nd	BOMB	BOVINGDON, PODINGTON
93rd	BOMB	ALCONBURY, BUNGAY, HARDWICK
94th	BOMB	BURY ST EDMUNDS
95th	BOMB	HORHAM
96th	BOMB	SNETTERTON HEATH
97th	BOMB	GRAFTON UNDERWOOD, POLEBROOK
100th	BOMB	THORPE ABBOTTS
301st	BOMB	CHELVESTON
303rd	BOMB	MOLESWORTH
306th	BOMB	THURLEIGH
310th	BOMB	BUNGAY
313th	TROOP CARRIER	FOLKINGHAM
314th	TROOP CARRIER	SALTBY
315th	TROOP CARRIER	ALDERMASTON, SPANHOE
316th	TROOP CARRIER	COTTESMORE
322nd	BOMB	ANDREWSFIELD and...

GROUP	ROLE	AIRFIELD(S)
322nd	BOMB	BURY ST ED', RATTLESDEN
323rd	BOMB	EARLS COLNE
339th	FIGHTER	FOWLMERE
344th	BOMB	STANSTED
351st	BOMB	POLEBROOK
352nd	FIGHTER	BODNEY
353rd	FIGHTER	METFIELD, RAYDON
354th	FIGHTER	BOXTED, LASHENDEN
355th	FIGHTER	STEEPLE MORDEN
356th	FIGHTER	MARTLESHAM HEATH
357th	FIGHTER	LEISTON
358th	FIGHTER	HIGH HALDON
359th	FIGHTER	EAST WRETHAM
361st	FIGHTER	BOTTISHAM, LITTLE WALDEN
362ND	FIGHTER	HEADCORN, WORMINGFORD
363rd	FIGHTER	STAPLEHURST
364th	FIGHTER	HONINGTON
365th	FIGHTER	BEAULIEU, GOSFIELD
366th	FIGHTER	THRUXTON
367th	FIGHTER	STONEY CROSS
368th	FIGHTER	CHILBOLTON
370th	FIGHTER	ANDOVER
371st	FIGHTER	BISTERNE
373rd	FIGHTER	WOODCHURCH
379th	BOMB	KIMBOLTON
381st	BOMB	RIDGEWELL
384th	BOMB	GRAFTON UNDERWOOD
385th	BOMB	GREAT ASHFIELD
386th	BOMB	BOXTED, GREAT DUNMOW
387th	BOMB	CHIPPING ONGAR, STONEY CROSS
388th	BOMB	KNETTISHALL
389th	BOMB	HETHEL
390th	BOMB	FRAMLINGHAM
391st	BOMB	MATCHING
392nd	BOMB	WENDLING
394th	BOMB	BOREHAM
397th	BOMB	HURN, RIVENHALL
398th	BOMB	NUTHAMPSTEAD
401st	BOMB	DEENETHORPE

GROUP	ROLE	AIRFIELD(S)
404th	FIGHTER	WINKTON
410th	BOMB	GOSFIELD
405th	FIGHTER	CHRISTCHURCH
406th	FIGHTER	ASHFORD
409th	BOMB	LITTLE WALDEN
416th	BOMB	WETHERSFIELD
434th	TROOP CARRIER	ALDERMASTON, FULBECK
435th	TROOP CARRIER	LANGAR
436th	TROOP CARRIER	BOTTESFORD, MEMBURY
437th	TROOP CARRIER	RAMSBURY
438th	TROOP CARRIER	GREENHAM COMMON, WELFORD
439th	TROOP CARRIER	BALDERTON, UPOTTERY
440th	TROOP CARRIER	EXETER
441st	TROOP CARRIER	LANGAR, MERRYFIELD
442nd	TROOP CARRIER	FULBECK, WESTON ZOYLAND
445th	BOMB	TIBENHAM
446th	BOMB	BUNGAY
447th	BOMB	RATTLESDEN
448th	BOMB	SEETHING
452nd	BOMB	DEOPHAM GREEN
453rd	BOMB	OLD BUCKENHAM
457th	BOMB	GLATTON
458th	BOMB	HORSHAM ST FAITH
466th	BOMB	ATTLEBRIDGE
467th	BOMB	RACKHEATH
474th	FIGHTER	WARMWELL
479th	ANTI-SUBMARINE	DUNKESWELL
479th	FIGHTER	WATTISHAM
482nd	BOMB	ALCONBURY
486th	BOMB	SUDBURY
487th	BOMB	LAVENHAM
489th	BOMB	HALESWORTH
490th	BOMB	EYE
491st	BOMB	METFIELD, NORTH PICKENHAM
492nd	BOMB	NORTH PICKENHAM
493rd	BOMB	DEBACH
495th	FIGHTER TRAINER	ATCHAM
496th	FIGHTER TRAINER	GOXHILL, HALESWORTH
801st	BOMB	HARRINGTON

In July 1944 Princess Elizabeth visited the 306th Bomb Group at Thurleigh, near Bedford, where she named a B-17G 'Rose of York' by smashing a carefully-shrouded bottle of Champagne against a panel attached to the chin turret guns. The 306th's CO, Colonel Claude Putnam, officiated and took her for a tour of Station 111. The Fortress was Seattle-built 42-102547 which was issued to the 306th's 367th Bomb Squadron in May 1944, taking the codes 'GY-F'. On a raid to Berlin on February 3, 1945 'Rose of York' was hit by flak and while limping back to base crashed into the English Channel, killing all ten on **board**. COURTESY 306th BOMB GROUP MUSEUM